11-90

As a New Day Breaks

A Contemporary View of Mashiach and Israel's Redemption

By: Rabbi Eliyahu Touger

Published by:
S. I. E. / E. M. E. T.
788 Eastern Parkway
Brooklyn, New York 11213
(718) 778-5436
Fax (718) 735-4139

Published and Distributed by

S. I. E.
788 Eastern Parkway
Brooklyn, New York 11213
Telephone: (718) 778-5436

5753 • 1993

ISBN 1-8814-0001-8

TABLE OF CONTENTS

ב״ה

PUBLISHER'S FOREWORD

As billboards and bumper stickers tell us "*Mashiach* is on the way," America and the world at large have responded with interest. The amount of news copy devoted to the issue is staggering — at one point, as many as 700 articles in a single week.

In this instance, the media is reflecting rather than directing people's interest. The subjects of *Mashiach* and the Era of the Redemption have attracted the public's attention. Lectures and symposia on these issues have begun to feature frequently in Jewish — and secular — communities around the world.

It has becomes obvious that the world is undergoing a transition of awesome scope. Revolutions in the geopolitical sphere are paralleled by radical changes in economics, communication, education, health, and community relations. Existing frameworks on the local, national, and international levels are giving way to new definitions.

Few noticed the start of the process, but now everyone is wondering where it will end. More and more people have come to the conclusion that the "birth pangs" we are experiencing preface the ultimate redefinition of society that will be brought into focus by *Mashiach's* coming. It is not surprising that in the past year and a half, more books and articles have been published about *Mashiach* and the Era of the Redemption than in the previous decade.

This material has reflected the entire spectrum of human belief — from sarcastic news copy questioning the very notion that a *Mashiach* could exist, to texts which accept as a given the premise that his coming is one of Judaism's principles of faith.

This book is not confined to a single approach or point of view. To explain: When the Lubavitcher Rebbe *Shlita* initiated his campaign to spread observance of Judaism's basic precepts, one of the mentors of his chassidim, Reb Mendel Futerfas, told the following story:

A salvage company once discovered a ship with an extremely valuable cargo sunk off the Baltic coast. It tried to lift the vessel with a crane, but the portion to which divers attached the cable broke off before the wreck could be raised. Finally, it was decided that instead of attaching a cable to only one place, balloons would be tied all over the ship's surface. As those balloons were inflated, they pulled the ship as a whole from its mire.

The purpose of this book is to attach thought balloons, as it were, to various parts of the public's consciousness, so that everyone — even those who do not accept these concepts on faith — will find points at which they can "tie in" to Mashiach and Redemption. As the "inflation" of these balloons generates awareness, speculation, interest and, finally, action, we can lift the ship — the entire world on which we are traveling — to a higher plane.

An attempt to reach out to all people is fundamentally related to Mashiach's coming. For the Redemption he will initiate is destined to affect everything. It will involve Creation as a whole, enabling each person — and indeed, every entity — to reach a level of fulfillment beyond its individual self.

The composition of this text reflects a combined effort by many people. The full list is too long to be recorded, but at the very least I would like to mention Uri Kaploun, whose expertise and counsel enhanced the elegance and style of the text; Gershom Gale, who edited the material; Yosef Yitzchok Turner, who is responsible for the graceful layout and typography; and Rabbi Yonah Avtzon, director of Sichos In English, whose assistance and encouragement at every stage helped transform a dream into reality.

We do not want the ideas presented to be accepted blindly. What we hope is that they encourage creative thinking about three points: a) the waves of change sweeping through our society; b) the imminence of the Redemption; and c) the idea that these two movements are interrelated.

When people start thinking about these concepts — hopefully before they have time for extended contemplation — Mashiach will arrive.

Eliyahu Touger

Jerusalem
28 Sivan, 5753

In Dedication

*To the Lubavitcher Rebbe Shlita,
who for 91 years has dedicated his life
to making the Redemption a reality.
May G-d grant him the health and
well-being to see that mission to its
conclusion, and may we and the
entire Jewish people join in
celebrating the Redemption in the
immediate future.*

CHAPTER 1:

FOCUS ON PROGRESS

We are living in unique and exciting times. Changes of a breathtaking nature are taking place, altering the structure of whole societies, and of our individual lives. This book is written for those people who welcome and encourage such changes, with the intent of clarifying the mindset and the goals that will empower us to proceed through these transitions with responsibility, purpose, and direction.

Our society is in a state of flux. The structures of life with which we are familiar are giving way to new systems, as evidenced by the collapse of communism and the re-thinking of capitalism, the breakup of nations, the melding of the planet into one economic whole, and the explosion and merging of previously discrete bodies of information.

This momentous overturning of things can be seen as indicative of a spiritual evolution. We stand at the threshold of the Redemption, the era of Messianic fulfillment promised by Israel's Prophets and the Talmudic Sages. Indeed, we are in the process of crossing that threshold.

How do we act in such an environment? Let's share two stories:

When NASA first began to consider the possibilities of extended space travel, its scientists decided to experiment with the effects of weightlessness on plants. Several seedlings were sent aloft in one of the first satellites.

The seedlings were in space for several months. Everything was structured to provide them with optimum conditions for growth. When the satellite returned, the biologists were amazed at the results; they had never seen plants like this before. Roots were growing out from every side. In several places, a stem had started to grow, only to have its growth aborted; leaves had sprouted at random. The researchers came to an obvious conclusion: When plants do not have up and down clearly defined for them, they don't grow correctly.

The second story takes place in a very different setting. Reb Mendel Futerfas was held for 14 years in Soviet prisons and labor camps. During this time, he spent most of his free hours in prayer and study. Nevertheless, he chose not to remain totally aloof from the gentiles who shared his lot, and spent a few hours each day conversing with them.

Included in this group were many types of people: political idealists who had fallen out of favor with the Stalinist regime, businessmen who had run undercover private enterprises, and ordinary people jailed for crimes the criminal nature of which neither they nor many of those who arrested them understood.

Among the latter was a circus performer whose claim to fame was his skill as a tightrope walker. He and Reb Mendel had a standing argument. Reb Mendel could not understand why a person would risk his life walking on a rope several storeys above the ground (for this was before safety nets had become standard circus practice).

"There must be," Reb Mendel maintained, "some hidden cables to hold you in case you slip."

For his part, the tightrope walker maintained that there was no need for cables. "It is not all that dangerous," he said. "One begins practicing on low ropes, and having gained experience, the risk of falling is minimal."

The argument continued until after Stalin died, and the prison authorities relaxed their rules. Several months before May Day that year, the guards told the prisoners that they would be allowed to prepare a makeshift circus to celebrate the day. Our acrobat suddenly came alive, becoming the center of attention. He organized various performances, the highlight being his tightrope walk.

He made sure Reb Mendel was in the audience. After the other acts were completed, the drums began to roll. He climbed the pole to the rope. His first steps were timid — after all, it had been several years — but within a few seconds, it all came back to him.

He began to twirl a hoop with his hands and wave to his friends. As he neared the end of the rope, he hesitated for a moment, made a fast turn, and then proceeded to the other side. On his way back, he exuded confidence; he performed several stunts and caught hats thrown to him. Completing his act, he climbed down and ran to Reb Mendel.

"You see, no cables holding me up," he gleamed in satisfaction.

"Yes. You're right, no cables," agreed Reb Mendel.

"You're a smart man," the performer continued. "Tell me. What's the secret? Is it in the hands? The feet?"

Reb Mendel paused to think. The performer had moved his hands freely, and it did not appear that his footwork was the determining factor.

After reviewing the scene in his mind several times, Reb Mendel replied: "It's the eyes. At all times, your eyes were riveted on the opposite pole."

The performer nodded in agreement. "When you see your destination in front of you, you know where to put your feet.

"And what is the most difficult part of the process?" he asked Reb Mendel.

Reb Mendel thought again and replied, "the turn."

"That's right," agreed the performer. "For then, you lose sight of the first pole and the other has not yet come into view."

Topsy-turvy conditions, the appearance of sudden turns, and the loss of familiar landmarks have become the rule and not the exception in our society. We appear to be living in a period of general discontinuity. Today, in all areas — politics, science, economics, and health — things look uncertain. Chance and change have become intermixed. Titles like "The Age of Unreason" and "Thriving on Chaos" are bestsellers even in the sedate business market. We are told to apply "upside-down thinking" to succeed in a society that refuses to allow us the time to stand still.

What is happening? In previous generations, sweeping change took time. Forecasts for the future were made with assurance; things were predictable. In the past century, and particularly in recent decades, advances in science, travel, and communications increased the rate of change. The introduction of the microchip and computerized systems of data management accelerated the rate of change so radically that it has gone off the graph.

Moreover, it is not only the rate of change that is unique, it is the nature of the changes that are occurring. The majority of us grew up with a Newtonian concept of the universe. This means that readily discernible causes are seen to produce predictable effects — a "clockwork universe." This vision spurred the Industrial Revolution, and enabled Western ideas and methods to attain a dominant position in world thinking.

Einstein's Theory of Relativity hinted at the existence of a higher degree of interrelation. People began thinking of non-linear systems, i.e., systems whose organization is not predictable in terms of the information within our grasp at any given moment.

This line of thinking has spawned a new theoretical approach referred to as the mathematics of chaos. Generally, we conceive of chaos as confusion or disorder. This new approach understands that what may be chaos to us is nonetheless the reflection of a hidden order motivated by a deeper and more abstract reality. Complex behavior appears random, and yet conforms to a pattern. For large, dynamic systems are organized according to different structures than those perceptible by our ordinary conceptual paradigms.[1]

---

1. Among the corollaries to this concept is the renowned butterfly effect; i.e., that the fluttering of a butterfly's wings in Singapore affects the weather in Michigan.

In previous generations, our lives followed more clearly mapped-out routines, and so we had less difficulty charting our future. But now, these maps are continually being redrawn, for the shifting reality in which we are living upsets our existing frameworks of reference. In such an environment, how does a person prevent himself from becoming as disoriented as our weightless plants? — By having the tightrope walker's sense of direction and purpose.

A person who knows where he is going knows where to put his feet. When the leader of a desert caravan or a ship's captain was unsure of the direction in which he was going, he would look into the night sky and find the North Star. As civilization advanced, the compass was invented.

A person who has an inner sense of purpose has a needle constantly pointing him true-north.

What is meant by inner purpose?

A person once complained of depression. Nothing in particular was wrong. On the contrary, both at home and at work, he was considered moderately successful, but as he approached 40, he was haunted by feelings of futility.

A friend told the present Lubavitcher Rebbe *Shlita* of the problem and the Rebbe advised him: "Share this insight of our Sages[2] with your friend: 'I was created solely to serve my Creator.' "

It made a difference. The person's attitude changed. After he saw the pole, he learned where to put his feet.

This insight is augmented by a classic Chassidic narrative involving the present Rebbe's ancestor, Rabbi Shneur Zalman

---

2.   *Kiddushin* 4:13.

of Liadi:[3] When Rabbi Zalman began to spread Chassidism throughout Russia, the government thought he wanted to lead a revolution against the Czar; Rabbi Zalman was arrested and held for questioning.

As the interrogation went on, many Russian officials were impressed by his wisdom, and arranged informal meetings with Rav Zalman. One of these officials, the Minister of Culture, was a learned man who had studied the Torah. He had a question.

"Why," he asked, "when G-d came to punish Adam after he ate from the Tree of Knowledge, did He ask him 'Where are you?'[4] G-d is omniscient. Why did He have to ask Adam where he was?"

Rabbi Zalman looked the minister in the eye and told him: "The Torah is eternal. G-d's question to Adam is addressed to every man, at every point in his life. At all times, G-d is asking us: 'Where are you? What are you doing to fulfill your purpose in life?'

"For example, you are so and so many years old [Rabbi Zalman mentioned the minister's exact age, although he had no ordinary way of knowing it]. G-d comes to you and asks you: 'Where are you in your mission in life? Do you know what you are expected to accomplish?' "

Deeply moved, the minister was very helpful in clearing the sage of the charges for which he had been arrested.

When we have the courage to look at ourselves honestly, we gain inner power and a handle on our future. When we consider our spiritual purpose, we encourage inner dynamism. We insure that this future will not be self-oriented, and thus

---

3.   *Likkutei Sichos*, Vol. I, *Yud Tes Kislev*, p. 73 ff.
4.   *Genesis* 3:9.

tap a source of energy higher and more potent than that con-
tained in our individual being.

Our Sages[5] describe every person as an entire world, and
the world as a personality in macrocosm. Conceiving of ourselves as a world, i.e., multifaceted and multi-dimensional,
enables us to develop harmony between and within the different aspects of our beings. Conversely, viewing the world as a
macrocosm of man also provides us with constructive insights.
**Just as an inner sense of spiritual purpose is the key to an
individual's success and happiness, so too the world at large
will thrive from gaining awareness of its spiritual purpose.**

What is the purpose of the world? Our Sages state:[6] "The
world was created solely for *Mashiach*." More specifically, they
tell us[7] that G-d created the world because He desired a dwelling among mortals. This implies that the infinite dimensions of
G-dliness will be revealed within the finite framework of
material reality.

These concepts are reflected in the world's cultural history.
In the first phases of human development, mankind knew no
boundary between the physical and the spiritual. Spiritual
concepts were interpreted in material terms, and man's conception of reality was a mixture of fact and fantasy. Slowly, scientific thought began to take hold, progressing to the
Newtonian concept of existence mentioned above. Man began
to appreciate the framework of existence in which he lived, and
learned how to function more efficiently within it.

As the time for *Mashiach's* coming draws near, Infinity has
begun to enter our conceptual frameworks. Or rather, our conceptual frameworks have begun to appreciate the Infinite. We

5. *Sanhedrin* 37a.
6. *Ibid.* 98b.
7. *Midrash Tanchuma, Parshas Bechukosai,* sec. 3. See the chapter entitled "The
Biggest Question of All" which focuses on this concept.

are witnessing an explosion of knowledge in all fields, introducing non-linear frameworks of reference that are mind boggling. The *Kabbalah* predicts[8] such a blossoming of thought, and teaches that this will prepare the world for the Era of Redemption.

Augmenting our awareness can precipitate these changes. The first step in this direction is a change in mindset, for ideas and information are the forces molding our society today. A revolution in thinking will send ripples of change throughout the world.

To speak in metaphoric terms: Ships have long been guided by the movement of a rudder. As ships grew larger, the rudders necessary to turn them also increased in size. Moving these larger rudders became difficult. Therefore, a small rudder referred to as the trim-tab was attached to the large rudder. This smaller rudder is easier to move; it then moves the large rudder, which in turn changes the course of the entire ship. In today's world, each of us can be such a trim-tab. The direction in which we point our lives can thus affect the direction of the vessel that is humanity.

Living with the Redemption[9] on a conceptual level, learning about the ideals which G-d envisions for our world, and integrating these principles in our lives, can serve as a trim-tab for every individual, channeling the direction of global change. By anticipating the Redemption in our minds and lives, we can precipitate its coming.

---

8.   *Zohar*, Vol. I, p. 117a. See the chapter entitled "The Blossoming of Knowledge" which elaborates on this idea.
9.   See the essay of this title in *Sound the Great Shofar* (Kehot, 1992).

Chapter 2:

A Sunrise Picture of Economics

When speaking of *Mashiach* and the Redemption, Maimonides does not mention an apocalypse, but a gradual process of growth and change. This revolution-by-evolution is perhaps nowhere more evident than in world economics.

Remember the coming of photocopy machines? Credit cards? Automated bank tellers? Data banks? Satellite Communications? Faxes? Each advance, if it was noticed at all, went by with a small sigh of "Oh, this is more convenient, isn't it?"

And then: A tourist checks into a hotel in Moscow. He pays with an American credit card, verified by direct line to an office in Belgium which shares a computer link to his bank in the States.

Moments later, a Japanese businessman representing a combined venture with an American company checks in. His credit check goes in the other direction, to Japan and across the Pacific. In less than five minutes, without the slightest departure from routine, two financial transactions span the globe.

Business as usual.

Suddenly, a single-world economy is in sight. The technology is here. International finance has already transcended the single-nation economies of the past. Take a look at the Ford Escort, a car being produced in the U.S., Britain, and Germany. Its component parts are made in Spain, Italy, Japan, and Brazil. And in Italy, a new resort complex is being built by South Korean workers with American management personnel.

Is there a deeper message behind these changes in the world's economic fabric? Why can't we see in the interlocking of national economies a backdrop for the environment of affluence, unity and peace that will characterize the Era of Redemption?

Because things are not perfect, economic might is still being abused to subjugate or to reward, and the industrialized nations are still learning the hard way that unless every one wins, every one loses. But the change is happening.

The creation of a unified global society is already within our conceptual grasp and, indeed, is already operating in a far more encompassing manner than we realize. Consciously or unconsciously, our personal and business lives have become dependent on international economic systems which less than 30 years ago would have been considered mere pipe dreams.

But most of us are far too busy hacking our way through the financial forest of day-to-day life to think much about the larger picture. If we think about *Mashiach* in economic terms at all, it is in a much more limited way…

About a week after the wedding, Yaakov Chayim began to speak with his new son-in-law about where to invest his dowry. The father-in-law offered advice, but the son-in-law was adamant. "I'm investing with Moshe David. He's promised me a high return; he's trustworthy. This is an opportunity I can't afford to miss."

Some months passed. Suddenly, the *shtetl* received a shock. Moshe David had gone bankrupt!

Unable to control himself, Yaakov Chayim rushed to his son-in-law's home.

"I'm glad you came," the son-in-law greeted him. "Now, I'd like to hear your investment advice."

"Investment advice?!" Yaakov Chayim said, his mouth agape. "What do you have to invest now?"

"My dowry," his son-in-law answered with a smile. "To get my money back from Moshe David before the investment was due, I had to sacrifice the interest, but the principal is still intact. Now, I have to reinvest it."

"How did you get your money back from Moshe David?" asked Yaakov Chayim incredulously. "He's bankrupt."

"Two weeks ago, I sensed something was going wrong, and I began to press him for my money. Five days ago, he gave me everything."

"But how did you know? How were you able to assess his financial status?"

"Believe me, I know nothing about finance," laughed the young man. "But I was standing next to him in *shul* and I heard him praying for *Mashiach* with great fervor. That was enough for me!"

The Prophets[1] speak of the Era of Redemption as a time when "the plowman shall overtake the reaper, and the treader of grapes he who sows the seed." To quote Maimonides:[2] "Good things will flow in abundance, and delights will be as freely available as dust."

Already today, such limitless bounty is a real possibility.

Let's take a look at the following figures in the United States. At the turn of the century, one third of all Americans worked on farms. They were able to feed America's population and produce raw materials for industry, but there was little left for export. Today, the American population has grown tremendously, and only 3% work on farms. Nevertheless, this 3% produce enough food, not only for the entire population, but to export throughout the world.

And in manufacturing: Many countries have developed an industrial framework that provides the average man with comforts and conveniences previously enjoyed by only the most wealthy and pampered. More and more nations are reaching the point where in all areas — agriculture, health, industry, communications and travel — technology has provided standards of living undreamt of by previous generations. And with minimum wages and industrial efficiency doubling ever more rapidly, the effects of these breakthroughs is being felt in even the poorest nations.

Today the challenge in the industrialized and post-industrialized countries is not how to produce wealth but how to

---

1. Amos 9:13.
2. *Mishneh Torah, Hilchos Melachim* 12:5.

encourage its production by the rest of the world, and how to distribute it more justly in the meantime. Can we create a global society that provides its members with peace and security rather than violence and fear? What kind of education will create both the knowhow to keep us moving forward and the spiritual maturity to keep us moving in the right direction?

Let's go back to Maimonides: Before telling us that in the Era of the Redemption, "Good things will flow in abundance, and delights will be as freely available as dust," he tells us:[3]

> The Sages and prophets did not yearn for the Messianic era to... rule over the nations, or to be exalted by them, nor in order to eat, drink, and enjoy happiness. Their aspiration was to be free [to involve themselves in the study of] the Torah and its wisdom, without anyone to oppress and disturb them so that they would be worthy of [a portion in] the World to Come.

Prosperity can only serve as a means; it must never become an end unto itself. A million is a one followed by six zeros. To treat this concept homiletically, without the One, the zeros are zeros, of no worth whatsoever. Comfort and wealth are beneficial to man only if they allow a life of wisdom, governed by spiritual values.[4]

Significantly, the ideals espoused by Maimonides are fast becoming principles that require practical application. The nature of our economy is minimizing the amount of human input required. To cite only one factor: The use of robots and sophisticated computers is being deliberately restrained because of their influence on the labor market. Should these restraints be withdrawn, even conservative estimates speak of a reduction

3. Op. cit.:4.
4. See the chapter entitled "The Blossoming of Knowledge" which highlights the need for an interrelation between knowledge and spiritual values.

of our work force by one third. Some people speak of 75% unemployment.

What will people do with their time? A person who anticipates the Redemption, and for whom *Mashiach* is a reality, knows that this time should be used to grow in understanding and awareness. The way to wisdom is a journey without end.

World prosperity will also change our interpersonal relationships. At present, people feel wealth to be scarce, and security rare. Naturally, this causes them to rationalize selfishness in the present so as to be sure of comfort in the future, to "look out for number one," and grab "their share of the pie." Needless to say, this breeds jealousy and lack of trust. It leads to corporate fraud and the attraction of "get-rich-quick" schemes. On a more basic level, it causes the violence and crime that plague our cities.

But what if the pie is big enough for everyone?

It is. It always has been; it's man that has been too small. This will be revealed in the Era of Redemption. Maimonides alludes to such a change in his words: "delights will be as freely available as dust."

Man will become conscious of the abundance of material blessings, and will no longer be obsessed by them. Since they will be freely available to all, people will partake of them whenever they desire, but without today's grappling for wealth and power. As Maimonides says:[5] "In that Era, there will be neither famine nor war, neither envy nor competition. Mankind will know hidden matters, and will attain an understanding of their Creator to the full extent of the human potential."

---

5.   *Loc. cit.*

CHAPTER 3:

THE BLOSSOMING OF KNOWLEDGE

Perhaps the most important change in the face of our society is the information revolution. Superior knowledge has become the hallmark of superior cultures, a dynamic force fueling our economies and inspiring creativity. And this is not merely an abstract matter, it is affecting every dimension of our lives. To cite the most obvious example: Probably 90% of the people reading this book are employed in either creating, processing, or selling information.

To better understand the role of knowledge today and in the future, it is worthwhile to take a brief lesson from the past: About 200 years before the Common Era, there were two cities in Western society renowned for their wisdom: Athens and Jerusalem. Athens produced poetry, philosophy, art, and drama. In Jerusalem, rabbis bent over scrolls studying the Law, thinking about how to apply that Law within the changing context of their contemporary experience.

Superficially, the Greek civilization looked more alive, more open-minded, more attuned to humanity. But an interesting thing happened when the two cultures interacted — the Greeks revealed an underlying narrowness and rigidity. When the Jews refused to adopt the Hellenistic lifestyle, the "liberal, enlightened" Greeks sought to destroy them, killing even mothers and babies because they wouldn't accept the allegedly superior Greek ideas and ideals.

Let's come closer to the present. At the turn of the 20th century, the world leader in philosophy, arts, and the sciences was Germany. Jewish wisdom had not disappeared, but was again viewed by many as more restricted, and perhaps a drop stale. The scrolls had been printed as books, and the number of books had proliferated, but the rabbis were still concerned with the same questions: What is the source from which a law is derived? And how can the Law be applied within the changing context of contemporary experience?

But as before, the culture which appeared more humane and advanced was built on the sands of pride. Its "wisdom," "knowledge" and "enlightenment" were all too easily perverted by the equally "human" and more compelling qualities of arrogance and brutality. Germany used its scientific knowledge to develop a fine-tuned murder machine which killed millions — attempting to offer a final solution to the questions confronting Jewish wisdom.

A clear message emerges. **Wisdom is not enough, not even wisdom with humanistic values.** Before it can serve as the basis for a synergistic society, human wisdom must itself be judged against the backdrop of an objective, external standard of good. And this standard must allow for the protection of wisdom, so that it cannot be abused by people or nations. **Wisdom can then reach beyond itself toward spiritual goals.**

At no time in history have these lessons been more relevant than today, for we are experiencing an explosion of knowledge that has placed previously undreamt-of power into human hands. Biotechnology, for example, is giving us access to the levers of Creation — the power to develop man and beast as we see fit. Or the power to kill billions.

This explosion of raw information has a price. Miraculous inventions go unseen because component A is in one discipline while component B is in another, and the scientists involved are too busy trying to keep abreast of advances in their own narrow field to be aware of what's being done in others.

The overwhelming sea of information submerges us, dwarfs our sense of self. How often have we met people who are struggling to feel their vitality, and who are challenged in their search for meaning and purpose?

As more and more of us are freed from manual labor, we are being given time to think. We all feel the need to live better lives. We want the wonders of technology to be balanced by a response to the spiritual demands of our human potential.

These needs are beginning to resonate throughout our society. In our schools we hear calls to change from educating for a particular task to educating for a lifetime of learning — not merely occupational training, but training for life, learning to be more human, to develop personal discipline, internal values, and integrity.

It is important to apply the lesson taught by the failure of the Greeks and Germans. Being merely human, we are imperfect. So in our quest to become fully human, we must strive for values that transcend humanity and search for the spiritual.

The *Zohar*,[1] the fundamental text of the *Kabbalah*, contains a stirring prophecy: **"In the six hundredth year of the sixth millennium, the gates of sublime wisdom will open and the wellsprings of lower wisdom will [burst forth, to] prepare the world to enter the seventh millennium."**

The six hundredth year of the sixth millennium began in 1839. The term "sublime wisdom" refers to the teachings of the Torah, and more particularly, to the mystic knowledge of the *Kabbalah*. "Lower wisdom" refers to secular knowledge, and "the seventh millennium" to the Era of Redemption, which like the Sabbath which follows the six ordinary days of the week, will be characterized by rest, comfort, and spiritual activity.

There is no need to elaborate on how the *Zohar's* prophecy has been fulfilled. We are all aware of the sweeping changes that have taken place since 1839. Advances in science and technology — the "bursting forth of lower wisdom" — produced the Industrial Revolution, and the post-industrial societies of today.

The *Zohar*, however, is emphasizing that these advances must proceed hand-in-hand with spiritual growth ("the sublime wisdom") if we are to avoid the grotesque errors of the past. Were we to focus solely on the lower wisdom, the progress achieved might enrich our pockets, but not our lives.

Recent decades have seen understanding of the Torah and its mystic dimension blossom. Where we have fallen short is in integrating the higher and lower spheres of knowledge. As we understand more about our environment, we must also understand more about ourselves, and the greater spiritual reality in which we live.

The *Zohar* stresses that the goal of both these paths of wisdom — the worldly and the sublime — must not be abstract

1.   Vol. I, p. 117a.

knowledge, or even individual enlightenment, but to bring mankind as a whole to a deeper, more complete realm of experience.

There is another aspect to the symbiotic relationship that exists between these two planes. Just as spiritual awareness complements our knowledge of the world around us, so too scientific knowledge can contribute to our conception of spiritual truth, allowing a more tangible understanding of these concepts. Take for example the Theory of Relativity: The notion that all existence is an interrelated flux of energy and matter can give us a more concrete understanding of how G-d's oneness permeates the universe.

Or take the following example: In 1987, a Canadian scientist working with a new tool to detect activity in the brain, discovered that the time it takes a signal to reach the cerebral cortex — that part of the brain which thinks — is always the same, regardless of age, sex or race. The time? Approximately 1/16 of a second.

The editor of the scientific journal which published this finding had been studying a tract of the Talmud[2] which focuses on the verse:[3] "G-d's anger lasts but a moment, His favor for life [eternal]." They ask: "How long is a moment?" and, through divine inspiration, arrived at the answer: 1/58888 of an hour, approximately 1/16 of a second. Our editor thought, "It seems that G-d's anger lasts for precisely the amount of time required for a human being to realize the fact."

Balanced progress in both the natural sciences and the sublime wisdom of the Torah will help transform the dream of an ideal future into a functional blueprint for society. It is impossible that it could be otherwise. For a future dependent on secular knowledge is a future based on the interaction of

2.   Berachos 7a.
3.   Psalms 30:6.

human minds. A future dependent on divine knowledge is a future based on the interaction of human souls. When human minds and souls interact, true communication can begin. And with true communication comes understanding. And with understanding comes compassion. And with compassion comes a natural movement towards universalism.

CHAPTER 4:

TO LEARN WAR NO MORE

Ours is not only an age of transition, but of paradox. On the one hand, we can see glimmerings of the peace, unity and prosperity of the Redemption. These, however, are only glimmerings; in actual life, things are very different.

Our Torah tradition explains that the time preceding the coming of *Mashiach* will be characterized by an enigma of this nature. We will experience a foretaste of the ultimate good of the Era of the Redemption.[1] At the same time, we will see a breakdown of values, and selfishness will prevail throughout society.[2]

---

1. See *Shelah*, Tractate *Shabbos*.
2. See the conclusion of Tractate *Sotah*.

Perhaps the most obvious expression of this paradox is the existence of war despite the universal desire for peace. War is nothing new. On the contrary, it appears to be a constant human condition. A short time after Creation, Cain killed Abel; half of humanity was involved in a conflict that destroyed one fourth of the world's population. Or, to take us a little further down the road of history, shortly after the first band of nomads decided to settle down and grow wheat, another band of nomads attacked them and raided their crops.

And, reading the newspapers, one might conclude that mankind has not really progressed since then. We've just gotten better at killing. Then they did it with rocks and clubs and now we have smart bombs, lasers, and atomic, chemical, and biological weapons in reserve if our conventional ones fail. On the other hand, we all desire peace. Moreover, the leading nations of the world have recently begun taking important strides in this direction.

Insight into this paradox can be gained through analysis of a passage from Maimonides' *Mishneh Torah*:[3] "There will be no difference between the current age and the Messianic Era, except [Israel's] subjugation to [gentile] nations."

But a few paragraphs later we read:[4] "In that Era, there will be neither famine nor war, neither envy or competition."

Don't these passages contradict each other? How can Maimonides tell us that the Messianic Era will not change nature, and yet say that men will no longer wage war?

---

3.   *Hilchos Melachim* 12:2. Similar statements are found in *Hilchos Teshuvah* 9:2, and in Maimonides' *Commentary on the Mishnah*, Introduction to ch. 10 of Tractate *Sanhedrin*. Maimonides' source appears to be *Berachos* 34b. See also the explanation of this concept and a discussion of miracles in the Era of Redemption in the essay entitled "Two Periods Within the Era of the Redemption," in *I Await His Coming* (Kehot, 1991).

4.   Ibid.:5.

The answer lies in the continuation of Maimonides' words:[5] "For good things will flow in abundance, and all the delights will be as freely available as dust."

The world will not change. Man will. Instead of using our intellectual and economic assets to create weapons of destruction, we will use them to enhance life. We will develop our resources successfully and enjoy abundance. Moreover, we will come to understand ourselves and our purpose in life much better. As a natural response, "They shall beat their swords into plowshares and their spears into pruning hooks. Nation shall not lift up sword against nation, nor shall they learn war any more."[6]

On the surface, such an approach makes so much sense. One cannot help wondering why mankind did not adopt it long ago.[7]

The answer is obvious. The perpetrators of war were concerned with their own immediate desires. Cain was envious of G-d's recognition of Abel; one group of nomads wanted the other's wheat; one nation wants another's oil. A country that goes to war decides it is simply going to take what it wants. For the winner, war pays.

But in the Era of Redemption, "delights will be as freely available as dust." We will all enjoy an abundance and indeed, an over-abundance of good things. Therefore, just as man does not crave dust, we will no longer lose our equilibrium in the

---

5. *Ibid.*
6. *Isaiah* 2:4.
7. This is not to say that we must adopt a policy of pacifism at all costs. On the contrary, there are wars that must be fought, but they are defensive in nature. When there are no more aggressors, even these wars will not be necessary.

lust for material benefits.[8] There will no longer be anything to gain by going to war.

An intimation of this process of **peace through prosperity** can already be seen. In the next decade, the likelihood of military conflict between Japan and the U.S. is next to nil. Both sides simply have too much to lose. The same concept applies in Europe. The probability of armed conflict between the U.S. and the nations of Western Europe, or wars among these nations themselves, is likewise negligible. Why? Because the stakes are too high.

It is not merely that the winners will also lose, that immense damage and loss of life will result on both sides. Beyond that, such wars would destroy the underpinnings of the new global economy on which both sides have come to rely, and that will simply not be allowed to happen.

Where *will* war be permitted? In nations like Bosnia and Somalia, and others not sufficiently integrated into the world's economic structure. The industrialized nations do not understand how such wars damage them. In fact, they make money by selling weapons to both sides. And so these little wars are allowed to continue. For now. And not for all that long. As the nations of the Third World become integrated into the world's economic picture, it will be clear that even such wars are damaging.

The transition to world peace will not come about miraculously; the change will come about through a shift in our thinking. As *Mashiach* spreads knowledge throughout the world, war and conflict anywhere will be shunned as primitive and wasteful.

---

8.   See the chapter entitled "A Sunrise Picture of Economics," which discusses the prosperity and affluence that will characterize the Era of Redemption.

A utopian dream? No, it's a reality shaping itself from day to day. A look at the defense policies of the U.S. and the former Soviet Union provides a preview of how Isaiah's prophecy will come to pass. War for these nations has simply become too expensive, the potential losses too great, and other needs too pressing. So swords are being beaten into plowshares; governments are cutting defense budgets and directing the freed resources to agriculture and social reform.

And not a moment too soon. All over the world, people are realizing that the real winner of the Cold War is Japan. While the U.S. and the U.S.S.R. were devoting their trillions to the development and stockpiling of weapons, the Japanese were concentrating on education and trade. The economic and technological advances made by Japan while the superpowers' attention was directed toward national security have propelled that country into a preeminence with few if any parallels.

It is true that these lessons have not stopped people from killing each other in large numbers. As this book is being written, three or four mini-wars are being fought, and others are waiting like tinderboxes for a match to ignite them.

But our willingness to tolerate even such little wars is ending. The communications revolution has brought war into our living rooms. Watching the Gulf War was like watching the Super Bowl. We cheered our troops like hardrooting fans, happy to watch the planes and helicopters take off and knock out "targets."

But then something changed. One of those targets happened to be a bomb shelter, and suddenly the world saw that the "enemy" had human faces and human hearts. Yes, they had supported Saddam, consciously or unconsciously, but they were human and we felt very uncomfortable when we saw that their blood was as red as ours.

In other words, **economic self-interest and instant global communications are making war obsolete.**

True, in the smaller nations the obsolescence of war is not yet recognized. But that is because their conception of reality remains limited. These populations have yet to experience the benefits of the modern world, and learn its lessons. Until they do, they will continue to promote war and terrorism. It will take time, and perhaps the actual coming of *Mashiach*, before international peace will become a top-to-bottom reality.

On the other hand, we've come a long way from the days when it was the leading nations that waged war against each other. Affluence and education are making a difference.

There is another dimension to the link between knowledge and world peace. The very concept of Redemption serves as a force promoting change. Not only does the present international situation enable us to see glimmers of the peace which *Mashiach* will introduce; seeing these glimmers encourages movement towards such peace.[9]

The climate of the world is changing. People are tired of continual stress, and of politicians who tell them it's healthy. Man has a natural desire for peace and security; we want to live in an environment where growth and knowledge can flourish

---

9.   In this context, the Lubavitch campaign to heighten the awareness of *Mashiach* and the Redemption can be seen as a political force. There are few Americans — no matter what their faith or where they live — who have not come into contact with these ideas. And this spread of ideas precipitates change.

   There is a concept called spiritual causation. In that vein, the story is told (*Meah Shearim*, p. 28a) that, at times, the Maggid of Mezritch would deliver teachings which he knew his listeners could not understand so that the messages would be "drawn down into the atmosphere of the world." This would facilitate their comprehension by others at a later date.

   The intent here, however, is to "draw down" the much more tangible influence of public opinion. As people become more familiar with the concept of Redemption, they will seek to have these ideals reflected in the societies in which they live.

without danger. As awareness of *Mashiach* and the Era of Redemption becomes more widespread, these feelings will rise to the surface, and excuses for war will become fewer and fewer.

CHAPTER 5:

A CHILD SHALL LEAD THEM

Babies are back. In the 80s, fewer families had children, and families had fewer children. In the 90s, more and more families have discovered that raising children is one of the most satisfying of all human endeavors.

The Prophet Isaiah states:[1] "The wolf will dwell with the lamb, the leopard will lie down with the young goat... and a child will lead them." There is a connection between the trend back toward family and Isaiah's vision, because the simple faith and incessant creativity of children — their unwillingness to accept complacency — make them a driving force toward change in society.

---

1.   11:6.

About 13 years ago, my wife and I served as emissaries (*Shluchim*) for the Lubavitcher Rebbe *Shlita* in South Africa. With youthful energy and idealism, we were anxious to spread the vitality that the Rebbe had infused into Jewish life.

We arrived in November. South of the equator, the seasons are reversed, so our first major project was leading a summer camp in December. When we left the Lubavitch community in Crown Heights, the children had begun singing the song, "We want *Mashiach* now; we don't want to wait." The Rebbe had encouraged the singing of this song, explaining that children intuitively feel something is lacking in their lives because *Mashiach* has not yet come.[2] We thought it important to teach this song to the children in our camp.

Now, 13 years ago in Capetown, the very concept of *Mashiach* was foreign. I doubt if the children there had ever heard the word. First, we taught the song to the counselors (most of them youths from Johannesburg who had a deeper connection to Judaism) and then we intended to teach it to the children.

My wife was to teach the girls. Because of the unfamiliarity of the subject, she had planned to introduce the song with a story and parable. But as she walked into the lunchroom, she was surprised to hear all the children singing "our song." The counselors had been inspired; they had taught it to the children, and the song had caught on.

My wife turned to one girl who was singing very loudly and asked: **"Who is *Mashiach*?"**

The girl replied: "I don't know, but I want him to come now."

---

2.   See *Sound the Great Shofar* (Kehot, 1992), p. 154.

How true this is for all of us! We all want *Mashiach* to come. Yet we do not fully comprehend what this would mean.

There are several levels to this concept. Once the followers of Rabbi Shneur Zalman of Liadi turned to him and complained: "Rebbe, we have been praying so hard for *Mashiach*, and still G-d has not sent him."

The Rebbe answered: "Maybe the *Mashiach* you are praying for is not the one G-d wants to bring."

What the Rebbe meant was that often we look forward to *Mashiach's* coming for personal reasons: to cover the overdraft in the bank, to resolve personal difficulties, or even to help us advance spiritually. G-d's concept of *Mashiach* involves the fulfillment of the ultimate purpose of Creation — the establishment of a dwelling for Him in this material world.

On a deeper level, the inability to comprehend *Mashiach* or the Era of Redemption is not a shortcoming; it is an inevitability. In the Era of Redemption, "Your Master will no longer conceal Himself, and your eyes will behold your Master."[3] G-dliness will be revealed without limitation. It is impossible for mortals to comprehend the matter in its entirety. Indeed, in regard to subjects of this nature, our Rabbis counsel that even scholars should try to match the simple faith of the child.[4]

For simple faith mirrors profound depth. G-d is totally above our mortal comprehension. We can neither know Him nor understand Him in the way we comprehend the material objects around us. In this context, our Rabbis say:[5] "The ultimate in knowledge is not to know." The Rabbis were not praising ignorance; they were pointing to the advantages of

---

3. *Isaiah* 30:20.
4. See *Rivosh*, Responsa 157, quoted in *Derech Mitzvosecha, Shoresh Mitzvas HaTefilah.*
5. *Sefer Halkrim*, R. Yosef Albo.

trust, belief and openness — qualities children possess in abundance — and explaining that these qualities allow us to relate to G-d's unlimited dimensions.

As we grow older, we should try to nurture these childlike qualities. One of the most abhorrent things is to see adults acting childishly. Yet one of the most attractive is to see them respond to a situation with the spontaneity, sensitivity, and energy of children.

The Grand Rebbe of Bobov was once sitting with his chassidim. As often happens at such a get-together, they ran out of refreshments. Immediately, a collection was made to purchase more. But who would go? None of the respected gentlemen was bestirred enough to trouble himself.

When the Rebbe saw the atmosphere of the gathering deteriorate as each tried to pass the responsibility to another, he told his followers: "Give me the money. I have a child waiting outside for me. He'll be happy to go to the store for us."

When the Rebbe failed to return shortly thereafter, the Chassidim realized that he had gone himself. Shamefacedly, they waited until he had completed the errand.

When he returned, they protested: "Why didn't you tell us the truth? If we had known you would go yourself, any one of us would have gone instead."

"I did tell you the truth," the Rebbe answered. "As I grew up, I resolved that I would never give up the childlike aspect of my personality. Needless to say, it is not always proper to act like a child. So when I sit with chassidim, I leave the child in me outside. But he is always waiting for me."

There is an intrinsic relationship between children and *Mashiach's* coming.[6] Our Sages tell us[7] that the Redemption from Egypt was dependent on the merit of righteous women. Despite Pharaoh's decree requiring Jewish boys to be drowned, these women bravely bore children and raised them as Jews. And our Rabbis assure us that the Redemption will come in the merit of righteous women who follow the example of their ancestors, bearing children and raising them as proud Jews.

Without endeavoring to fathom this process of spiritual causality, we can notice the radical changes being wrought by today's renewed desire for family. The '80s were referred to as the "me" decade. Not surprisingly, there was a rise in divorce and families had fewer children. Indeed, the entire concept of the nuclear family was challenged, and in many instances redefined. Now we are witnessing a swing back to more traditional mores. There is a greater desire for lasting marriage. Couples are deciding to have more children, and to spend more time with them.

But the desire to spend time together is not always enough. Even when parents love their children and genuinely care for them, they may have trouble building bridges of communication. The reasons are often obvious. When the most important family discussions are about how often to buy a car, and which television programs to watch, it is natural that a family will grow apart.

Why is there a generation gap? Not because parents and children don't care for each other, but because they have been educated to self-interest. When every member is concerned with his own personal benefit, it is natural that the family structure suffers. When the father stays late at the office, the mother is over-involved in her job or community work, and the

---

6. *Yevamos* 62a.
7. *Sotah* 11b. Similarly, *Yalkut Shimoni*, Vol. II, the conclusion of sec. 606, explains that subsequent redemptions also came about through the merit of women.

children have different social functions to attend, it is highly unlikely that they will be able to maintain a deep relationship. Without something to bind them together, they will sleep under the same roof, sit in the same living room, watch the same TV programs, and yet be worlds apart.

What can cement the relationship between parents and children? True values. When a family shares principles and values, its members have something which brings them together. The more lasting the values, the more powerful and permanent the bond.

By nature, people want to share, but are often clumsy in doing so. That clumsiness, however, can be overcome. Parents who stutter or have other difficulties expressing themselves often have powerful bonds with their children.

Nor does the difficulty lie in having something to communicate. Every person has a host of experiences rich with meaning and value.[8] What matters is the ability to select the experiences to communicate, and in which context. This is where having genuine values and principles makes all the difference.

When a family shares a sense of mission and purpose, its members have a framework with which to guide and govern their responses to the world. This sense of vision is shared by all, and builds bridges across the generations. In such families, parents talk to their children until late at night. And children crowd around their grandparents listening to stories. The whole family gets together for evenings of shared reminiscences, song, and laughter.

---

8.   See *Kiddushin* 33a which explains that great Sages would show respect to vintage gentlemen. Even if the elderly are lacking in the knowledge gained from books, the wisdom that they have culled from their life experience makes them worthy of respect.

There is an old Yiddish adage which says: "More than Israel has kept the Shabbos, the Shabbos has kept Israel." The closeness established around the Shabbos table provides the dynamism that has made the Jewish family an ideal looked up to by other cultures.

(Important by-products of such a relationship are the dignity it restores to old age and the great resources of experience that this dignity makes available to other family members. What's the difference between a revered elder and an old fogy? The former stands for something, and his children and grandchildren share his purpose.[9])

The greater the purpose and the deeper the values shared, the more powerful the bond connecting family members to each other. This is one lesson of the song we mentioned. When children feel a lack in their lives because *Mashiach* has not come, they and their parents — when these sentiments are shared by the family as a whole — are focusing on the most meaningful of values, the very purpose of Creation.

Perhaps this is implied in the verse:[10] "Behold I will send you Eliyah[u] the prophet before the coming of the great and awesome day.... And he shall turn the heart of the fathers to the children." The prophet is telling us that "the great and awesome day," the coming of Redemption, will be heralded by families coming together. Focusing on the imminence of that day and cultivating the awareness that we are on the threshold of understanding will enable parents and children to internalize these values.

Our Rabbis point out another important dimension of the verse. Rashi interprets it to mean, "He will turn the hearts of

9. In regard to this dimension, see the essay entitled "Torah, the Beauty of the Elderly," Sichos In English, Vol. 6, pp. 212 ff.
10. *Malachi* 3:23-24.

the fathers to G-d though the medium of the children."[11] In this time of transition, we can learn from our children.

Our Sages tell us[12] that it was the children who first recognized G-d at the crossing of the Red Sea. Similarly, in the Era of Redemption, it will be the children who first sense the nature of the times. The emphasis is not on the historical parallel. Quite the contrary, the parallel exists because there is an intrinsic connection between the perception of G-d's hand and the unique nature which children possess. For the inquisitiveness, creativity, and energy of children place them firmly in the present, with a focus on the future. They don't need lectures on the value of constant learning; their entire lives are directed toward assimilating new experiences.

Adults, by contrast, often allow their vitality to atrophy. We adopt textbook answers that no longer relate to actual experience. Even after we discover real answers, we often blindly repeat them until they in turn become mere routines, and this prevents us from continuing the growth that gave us those answers in the first place. It is only with the heart of a child that we can understand and put into practice the purpose of G-d.

---

11. *Loc. cit.* This interpretation stems from the fact that the Hebrew original states *al bonim* (על בנים) instead of the expected phrase *el bonim* (אל בנים).

12. *Sotah* 11b; *Shmos Rabbah* 23:8. Even the youngest infants joyfully joined in the song of redemption (*Sotah* 30b).

Chapter 6:

ETERNAL LAND, ETERNAL HOPE

Barely a day passes without the Land being in the head-lines. And barely a day passes without you and I looking at the small print to find out what's happening.

Two questions: Why does a small country with so little apparent economic influence or strategic importance dominate the news? And why are all Jews, religious and secular, so interested in events there?

The fact that *Eretz Yisrael*, the Land of Israel, features in the news so frequently is symptomatic of its prominent role in the process of change that is shaping the future. And the involvement and concern we feel for the Land indicates its deep connection with the core of our being. None of our peo-ple are casual about their relationship with the Land. Even when Israel is in no direct danger, the connection is alive, and any discussion about the political situation there is likely to be stormy.[1]

About 15 years ago, one of my friends was sent to awaken an awareness of Judaism in Russia. This was during the Brezhnev era, when such activities had to be carried out in secret, avoiding the ever-present eyes of government agents.

He met many Jews who had applied for exit visas to *Eretz Yisrael*, but whose requests were denied. From the time they made their application, opportunities to advance professionally were denied them, and often they would lose their jobs entirely. Nevertheless, with a tenacity that befits the children of "a stiff-necked people," they applied again and again.

My friend asked one of these refuseniks **how long he had been waiting to go to *Eretz Yisrael*.**

"For 2,000 years," the man answered.

The most important dimension of the story is its epilogue. **Last winter, I met the man in *Eretz Yisrael*.** His wish, and that of hundreds of thousands of his brethren, has finally been granted. He has settled into one of the suburbs of Jerusalem, and is learning Hebrew.

This is a unique period in history. **Dreams that are 2,000 years old are being consummated.** And this is merely a fore-taste of things to come.

---

1. Appreciating the existence of such a connection within all of our fellow Jews will facilitate the process of communication between the different factions of the Jewish community. No group has a monopoly on genuine concern for *Eretz Yisrael*. A Jewish radical who supports the PLO does so because *Eretz Yisrael* is important to him and this is his way of expressing his concern. When members of different factions appreciate that they share a kinship, they can share views more readily. When such an approach is adopted, even though a consensus is not reached, the differences that remain will be between brothers.

There is no way that anyone can view the return of the Jewish people to *Eretz Yisrael*, and the spreading of Jewish settlement throughout the Land, without feeling the imminence of Redemption.

Let's not fool ourselves. The Redemption is not yet a fact, and Jews in *Eretz Yisrael* have constant reminders that they too remain in Exile, the *Intifada* and the Scuds being only the latest. But that is only one dimension, and a secondary one. The fact that after 2,000 years, there are millions of Jews in *Eretz Yisrael*, that the deserts are blossoming and ancient cities are being rebuilt, that children laugh in the streets of Jerusalem, is a miracle made possible only because the time for Redemption is near.

Just how the present day should be described is a matter for debate: Should this ongoing miracle be called an intimation of the Redemption, a glance from afar, or should another term be used? The man in the street, both in *Eretz Yisrael* and in the Diaspora, has little interest in such abstractions. He knows about the travails the Jews endured journeying from nation to nation throughout the Exile, and feels that for our people as a whole, this stage is over; the Jews have returned to their homeland.

Why? It is not because the Land possesses a nice climate (though it does), nor because our people have created an exciting society there since their return (though they have). We care because *Eretz Yisrael* is part of our spiritual heritage. It is the home of our fathers' fathers' fathers, and of our children's children's children. Our Rabbis[2] tell us that every Jew possesses a portion in *Eretz Yisrael* — an actual piece of land.

---

2. There are *halachic* authorities (e.g., Responsa of Rabbeinu Meir ben Baruch, Responsa 536, *Otzar HaGeonim*, *Kiddushin*, sec. 146) which state that every Jew possesses four square cubits in *Eretz Yisrael*. Moreover, on the basis of this

And *Eretz Yisrael* possesses a portion of every Jew; a piece of our heart and soul.

On the other hand, within the present conditions, despite the connection we share with *Eretz Yisrael*, most Jews are not moving there just yet. Indeed, the majority of those who have made *aliyah* to *Eretz Yisrael* have come out of need, not out of desire. We are happy, or at the very least, familiar, with our present-day circumstances and do not want to exchange them for a new frame of reference that we fear will be too challenging.

This is one of the reasons the Reform movement originally struck out all references to *Eretz Yisrael* and the Redemption from its prayer book. They were concerned only with the here and now.

But after the Second World War, and to a greater extent after 1948, such an approach was no longer possible and the books were altered. Today, whether or not he makes *aliyah*, every Jew now realizes that what happens in *Eretz Yisrael* is happening to him.

And a lot has been happening. The sheer volume of news is staggering. The fact that the attention of the world is focused on *Eretz Yisrael* is not coincidental. **Eretz Yisrael is intended to be the center of world attention.**

The other nations, and perhaps many Israelis, may not be aware of the real reason. But time and again, the world is forced to notice that what takes place in *Eretz Yisrael* influences the whole planet.

The events occurring in *Eretz Yisrael* are not always pleasant. This is because we are still in Exile. For Exile is not merely

---

concept, these authorities apply certain principles of Jewish business law that are relevant only when a person owns real estate.

a geographic condition.[3] Quite the contrary, the fundamental characteristic of Exile is the blurred vision of the truth which it induces. The truth is not hidden entirely, but the way in which it is manifest requires substantial decoding.

Unraveling the messages of Exile and understanding their intent hastens the coming of the time when decoding will no longer be necessary. Our awareness of what *Eretz Yisrael* means will speed the coming of the time when "a great congregation will return there";[4] Jews from all over the world will stream to *Eretz Yisrael*, celebrating the Redemption.

---

3. For this reason, even Jews living in *Eretz Yisrael* recite "Because of our sins, we are exiled from our land..." (Festival *musaf* liturgy, *Siddur Tehillat HaShem*, p. 258) and other prayers reflecting our desire to return from exile.
4. *Jeremiah* 31:8. See Maimonides, *Mishneh Torah, Hilchos Melachim* 11:4, 12:1,5, which explains that in the Era of the Redemption, all Jews will return to *Eretz Yisrael* and live there in freedom, peace, and prosperity.

CHAPTER 7:

SEARCHING FOR LIGHT

Sedona is a small town nestled amid the red-rock canyons and cactus bushes of Arizona. Fifteen years ago, with the exception of a few experts on American Indians, nobody had heard of it. Today, Sedona is one of the leading tourist attractions in America, drawing approximately three million visitors a year. Tens of millions of dollars in revenue are generated annually.

What made the difference? An audio tape by a self-styled spiritualist which describes seven "vortexes of spiritual energy" located in the rock formations around the community. The tape spawned a new legend. People came searching for paranormal psychic phenomena, deeper spiritual experience, and some meaning and inner peace in their lives. In doing so, they made Sedona the "capital of the New Age."

The majority of these visitors are not '60s holdovers or East or West Coast intellectuals. Most are members of middle America: schoolteachers, retired businessmen, and veterinarians, the kinds of people who could be my neighbor or yours. They are not all under 40. Quite the contrary, among them are grandmothers and grandfathers.

And Sedona is not an isolated phenomenon. Over 25 million Americans, approximately one tenth of the nation's population, profess to be involved in New-Age spirituality — a combination of myth, mystery, and metaphysics which promises supernatural healing, one-on-one communication with G-d, and the development of extra-sensory perception.

What is at the core of this phenomenon? Loneliness. Overwhelmed by the torrent of raw data in our high-tech society, people are seeking to get back in touch with their human side. Even purely business-oriented books urge an attempt to balance the material advances of technology with the spiritual demands of human nature.

People want deeper meaning in their lives. They are seeking to reawaken a lost sense of community in their relations with others, and regain the inner security that comes from living with a spiritual purpose.

Such desires have kindled a greater sensitivity to spiritual awareness, with ramifications on many levels. To cite a conspicuous example: Even the most mainstream medical practitioners have come to appreciate the existence of a link between body and soul.

But there is a fundamental difficulty. This search for spirituality has a freelance, even entrepreneurial dimension to it. It is belief without structure, a supermarket of spiritual ideas lumped together, as individuals attempt to define spirituality in their own way.

And one cannot ignore the business aspect of it. Without mentioning the millions made by gurus and evangelists, the fact is that "how-to" books on personal growth and prepackaged spiritual awareness programs are big business. And a lot of that money is made by catering to people's weaknesses and insecurities; the spiritual "guides" know they are not providing real answers.

What's more, although the desire for community is a positive thing, in practice, it often covers a longing to be accepted easily, to be held in someone's arms, and to hold someone else, instead of having to compete in a cold society. And this "feel-good" sense of community often has little to do with authentic compassion or real personal sacrifice.

In short, the spiritual quest all too often becomes a search for the individual high, a catharsis of inner yearning instead of an ongoing, systematic process of development. In the 60s, members of the drug culture used to say that because Americans are such a materialistic people, G-d put spirituality into chemicals. Twenty-five years later, real progress has been made. On the whole, people are no longer depending on chemicals for spiritual highs, and have realized that growth must come from increased awareness. But still, this awareness is usually thought of as coming from above, descending upon us and bestowing unearned bliss.

Learn the lesson of the soda bottle: **No deposit, no return.**

We can't expect spiritual growth and awareness to come by itself. **A harvest cannot be reaped without sowing seeds.** There is no such thing as spirituality without sacrifice. Self-discipline, the courage to face oneself, and good old-fashioned work are keys to growth.

But they are not the only ones. One of the most frequently quoted stories in Jewish thought is Rabbi Yehudah HaLevi's tale of the Khazar king's dream.[1] The Khazars were a successful nation living in Mid-Asia. Their king wanted to develop the moral fiber of his people and advance himself spiritually. But every night he was haunted by a recurring dream. It was as if an angel was telling him: "G-d appreciates your intent, but not your deeds."

The dream spurred the king to even greater efforts. He studied and labored to improve his spiritual service. Nevertheless, he continued to receive the same message. So he invited sages from the world's three great religions to teach him the essence of their faiths, and ultimately took the never-ending path called Judaism.

The story teaches a profound lesson: A person can be willing, and can even make substantial sacrifices, but to borrow an expression from our Sages:[2] **"A man in fetters cannot set himself free."**

The realization that there exists an eternal, spiritual Truth beyond the limits of ordinary human experience is an important first step, but only if it prompts a second: To seek out a spiritual path that has proven its effectiveness over the course of time.

Seeking such direction is necessary, for by definition, there is a gap separating the material from the spiritual. As mortals, we know that the spiritual exists, and can even appreciate that we have a spark of it within us,[3] but in terms of our conscious experience, it is distant from us. On his own initiative, a finite man has no means to establish common ground with an infinite G-d.

---

1. *HaKuzari*, Discourse 1.
2. *Berachos* 5b.
3. See *Tanya*, ch. 2.

The nature of this schism and how to bridge it is the subject of a unique teaching of the *Midrash*:[4]

> King David taught: "The Holy One, blessed be He, decreed:[5] 'The heavens are the heavens of G-d, and the Earth He gave to men.'"
>
> To what can this be compared? To a king who decrees that the inhabitants of Rome may not descend to Syria, and the inhabitants of Syria may not ascend to Rome.
>
> Nevertheless, when [G-d] gave man the Torah, He nullified that decree and said: "The lower realms will ascend to the higher realms, and the higher realms will descend to the lower realms. And I will begin." As it is written:[6] "And G-d descended on Mount Sinai," and "to Moses He said: 'Ascend to G-d.'"

G-d "reached down" into the world, giving us His Torah so that we could establish a bond with Him. The large majority of the Torah's teachings focus, not on prayer or worship, but on agricultural laws, marriage, family, and business relations. And yet, "the Torah and the Holy One, blessed be He, are One."[7] **Even as it deals with the mundane realities of our material environment, the Torah is one with G-d.**

Thus by establishing a bond with the Torah, a person establishes a bond with his Maker. To borrow an analogy of our Rabbis,[8] it is like embracing a monarch. Although one feels the

---

4. *Shmos Rabbah* 12:3.
5. *Psalms* 115:16.
6. *Exodus* 19:20.
7. *Zohar*, Vol. I, 24a.
8. *Tanya*, ch. 4.

king's garments and not his actual flesh, one is nonetheless holding the king, and being held by him.[9]

Also significant is the *Midrash's* statement that it is G-d who says, "I will begin." The Torah is an incursion by G-d into man's world, for only that could make possible man's entry into G-d's.

The Torah is intended not merely to give man the opportunity of establishing a bond with G-d, but also to make the world G-dly, as our Sages stated:[10] "The Torah was given solely to refine the created beings." Thus we find a parallel between the Ten Commandments and the Ten Utterances of Creation. For the Torah is intended to permeate Creation, and connect it to G-dliness.[11]

In that context, we can understand our Sages'[12] division of the six millennia of recorded history into 2,000 years of chaos, 2,000 years of involvement with the Torah, and 2,000 years of [concern with] the Era of *Mashiach*. The Torah represents the eternal uplifting of all things ordered from all things chaotic — a medium through which man can find the pattern and establish meaning within the hubbub of material existence, and thus bring about the ultimate fulfillment that will characterize the Era of Redemption.

Moreover, **it is not only that the Torah was given to enable the world to blossom; it is in itself the blossoming.**

---

9. This concept is reinforced by an analysis of the Hebrew word used to refer to the observance of G-d's commandments, *mitzvos* (מצות). *Mitzvos* shares the same root as the Hebrew word *tzavta* (צותא) meaning "connection." For the purpose of the *mitzvos* is to establish a bond with G-d (*Likkutei Torah, Bechukosai* 45c).

10. *Bereishis Rabbah* 44:1.

11. See *Timeless Patterns of Time* (Kehot, N.Y., 1993), Shavuos, essay 1, which explains that by performing a *mitzvah*, one establishes an eternal bond between G-d and the material objects with which the *mitzvah* is performed.

12. *Sanhedrin* 97a.

Maimonides portrays the Era of Redemption as a time when the underlying goal of all human activity will be the perfect observance of the Torah and its *mitzvos*.[13] For this reason, after negating the notion that *Mashiach* must work miracles,[14] Maimonides writes:[15] "The essence of the matter is: This Torah, its statutes and its laws, are everlasting."

For the Torah is communication between G‑d and man. At present, we have only a limited awareness of the G‑dly truth the Torah conveys. In the Era of Redemption, its spiritual dimensions will be openly revealed, and the occupation of the entire human race will be solely to know G‑d.[16]

The Jews will take their place as "a nation of priests,"[17] and will know the hidden matters, attaining an understanding of the Creator to the full extent of human potential; as it is written:[18] "The earth will be filled with the knowledge of G‑d as the waters cover the ocean bed."

---

13. *Mishneh Torah, Hilchos Melachim*, ch. 11. See the essay entitled "The Function of *Mashiach*" in *I Await His Coming* (Kehot, 1991) where this concept is explained.
14. See the chapter entitled "Will *Mashiach* Work Miracles?" where this idea is developed.
15. *Loc. cit.*:3.
16. *Loc. cit.*:12:5.
17. *Exodus* 19:6.
18. *Isaiah* 11:9.

CHAPTER 8:

CHOSEN FOR WHAT?

Rabbi Spiro, the Bluzhever Rebbe זצ"ל, survived Auschwitz. Day after day, he saw new arrivals sent to the gas chambers. Day after day, he watched while mothers carrying infants were forced to line up and have their babies taken away from them, condemned to a crueler death than their mothers would find.

One day, he saw a woman in line with a young infant. With obvious anguish, she approached one of the German soldiers. "Do you have a knife?" she asked. Frantically, Rabbi Spiro ran toward her, wanting to tell her that whatever her fate or that of her baby, she should not injure herself or her child.

The Germans brutally restrained him, and with a sadistic grin, one soldier gave the woman a knife. She put her child to the ground, and held the knife over him. But she didn't slay him; she circumcised him.

"You gave me a beautiful Jewish child," she cried out, looking heavenward. "And I am returning him to You, perfect as You desired."

Circumcision is "a covenant in our flesh,"[1] a sign that the Jews are G-d's chosen people. But what are they chosen for?

Throughout history, our people have faced bitter oppression and persecution. And this has evoked a natural response: G-d! If this is what being Your chosen people means, please choose someone else!

But G-d doesn't. His covenant with the Jews is eternal and unchanging. And that's why time and again, this numerically insignificant people and the tiny Land of Israel have featured so prominently in world history.

And despite occasional protests, a Jew responds and chooses G-d.[2] Yes, he might intellectually object, for the concept of being part of a chosen people, different from those around him, is a difficult one. But what happens when someone calls him a dirty Jew? He reacts in proud affirmation of his Jewish identity!

Our people possess a glorious heritage of martyrdom which is centuries old. And this is not merely a relic of the past. The Holocaust occurred only 50 years ago. Less than five years ago, Jewish activists were being deported to hard-labor camps in

---

1.   *Genesis* 16:13.
2.   In *Tanya*, ch. 19, R. Shneur Zalman of Liadi writes that, by nature, a Jew cannot do otherwise. His fundamental Jewish core will not allow him to deny his connection with G-d and His Torah. "No Jew can — and no Jew will — separate himself from G-d."

In *Basi LeGani* 5710, chs. 3 & 4 the Previous Lubavitcher Rebbe explains that a person's conduct can dull his sensitivity so that on a conscious level, he may not realize when he is indeed living apart from his G-dly core and his Jewish identity. In every Jew, however, there is a point at which this spark will be aroused, and at that time, he will sacrifice everything in affirmation of his Jewishness.

Siberia for teaching their faith and spreading national awareness.

The tenacity of our people's connection to their Jewish identity is expressed in ways other than martyrdom. **The challenge is, after all, to live for our faith.** No Jew considers his Judaism a trivial matter. We speak of Irish, Italian, and black *Americans*, but of American *Jews*. For a Jew, Judaism is more than bagels, blintzes and latkes, or even a set of religious practices; it is a manifestation of who the person is. He is a Jew.

Toynbee called Judaism a fossil. The way Jews cling to their identity is surely anachronistic in the modern age, for our society is very much a melting pot. And this is becoming increasingly true as the outward differences between peoples and societies fade and we come to terms with the concept of a global village. Although today, ethnic and national diversity are celebrated, rather than shunned, clinging to one's Jewish identity is something different entirely.

A best-selling American book describing a Jew's confrontation with American life was called "The Chosen." A Frenchman would never choose such a title for a book that focuses on the differences between himself and an Italian or a German. When we say the Jews are G-d's chosen people, it implies a radically different identity — an identity linked to a purpose, one which is unique in the world.

And this points to a conceptual difficulty of a greater scope: In ancient times, each nation had a god or gods of its own. The Philistines had their gods, the Moabites had their gods, and the Egyptians, theirs. At that time, Judaism was unique, because the G-d of Israel was not an idol or a star like these tribal divinities, but rather an unseen spiritual power.

Abraham broke his father's idols. By writing down the words of the Torah and taking them throughout the world, our people taught mankind as a whole to break its idols. For the Torah introduced the Truth that underlies all philosophy, ethics and metaphysics, and thus enabled the world to emerge from tribal paganism. In Isaiah's words,[3] Israel was chosen to be "a light unto the nations; to open the blind eyes," communicating a message which the inhabitants of our world would not have been able to perceive otherwise.

Nevertheless, as this truth began to find acceptance in the cultures of our fellow men, and people began to speak of universal faiths, Judaism comes to occupy a paradoxical position. On one hand, it is still considered one of the world's major religions, a faith with a universal message. On the other, it remains very much a tribal faith, limited to the descendants of Abraham, Isaac and Jacob. Yes, converts are accepted,[4] but conversion is not encouraged. Judaism has never sent out missionaries. Instead, it has concentrated on educating its own.

Judaism's gifts of compassion, love, and faith permeate nearly every field of human activity, but because they have been given quietly, the nations can ask: "What have you done for us lately?" The Torah was given over 3,300 years ago. More particularly, since the completion of the Talmud (approximately 500 CE) when the spiritual truths of the Oral Law were recorded for posterity, what has Judaism been doing for mankind?

This question is particularly relevant in the present age, for we have witnessed a surge in religious consciousness throughout the world, and an even greater escalation is expected. In these times of turbulence and transition, the structure and order which religion inspires serves as a firm foundation on which people can base their lives.

---

3.   *Isaiah* 42:6-7.
4.   Indeed, a unique degree of respect and admiration has always been granted to converts. See the letter of Maimonides addressed to Ovadiah, the convert.

And this support is not necessarily a crutch. For the first time, science and mathematics have revealed multi-faceted systems of order in nature and society that strengthen rather than challenge a religious conception of existence. Moreover, the shallowness of secular consumerism is making it clear that only time-tested values should lie at the vortex of our lives.

Unfortunately, Judaism has not reaped the full benefits of this spiritual awakening. We have seen the growth of a large *teshuvah* movement which has brought thousands of Jews back to their religious roots. But their numbers, however great, are small when one thinks of the millions of Jews who still have only a minimal connection to their heritage. More than half of the Jewish children in America are not receiving any formal Jewish education at all. And when one thinks of the religious revival in the United States, it is Eastern mysticism, contemporary religious experiments, or the Southern Baptists that come to mind.

What then is Judaism's message for today?

To prepare the world for Redemption.[5]

To explain: In Judaism, matrimony is a two-stage process involving betrothal *(erusin)* and marriage *(nisuin)*. Betrothal establishes the husband-and-wife bond. From that time onward, a woman cannot marry anyone else, but neither may the couple live together. Marriage, by contrast, signals the consummation of this relationship, the beginning of the couple's life as a single unit.[6]

---

5. Significantly, the *Metzudas David* and other commentaries interpret the passage from *Isaiah* cited previously as referring to the communication of the message of Redemption.

6. Today, the common Jewish practice is to complete both stages of the wedding bond in a single ceremony under the wedding canopy.

Our Sages[7] explain that the giving of the Torah represented the betrothal; only in the Era of Redemption will the marriage of man and G-d be consummated. The giving of the Torah established the first connection between the spiritual and the material. This connection has, however, an element of distance, for life in our world remains materially oriented. It is only in the Era of Redemption that this bond will be consummated, and the awareness of spirituality will permeate our ordinary experience.

Thus, from the time Israel received the Torah, our task has been to prepare ourselves and the world for Redemption. One dimension of that task is reflected in our involvement in the material elements of worldly existence. For the G-dly life force which sustains the world is concealed within its material substance.

Chassidic thought[8] refers to this involvement with the Hebrew term *tziruf,* the word used to describe the smelting of ore. In the smelting process, the dross is discarded and the precious metal purified. Similarly, in our involvement with material concerns, our intent is to reveal the hidden G-dly energy vested in our physical reality.

Knowingly or unknowingly, willingly or unwillingly, the Jews have fulfilled this purpose as they wandered from country to country, tapping the G-dly energy invested in those lands by using their physical substance in the fulfillment of *mitzvos.* In the Era of Redemption, we will reap the harvest of our labors, for the knowledge of G-d will permeate every dimension of existence.

---

7. *Shmos Rabbah* 15:31; *Likkutei Sichos,* Vol. IX, p. 147, fn. 27* and sources cited there.
8. See *Sefer HaMaamarim 5702,* pp. 67-70 (cited at the beginning of *From Exile to Redemption,* Vol. I, Part 1, ch. 2, p. 29), and other sources.

Another element of Israel's task is sharing the Torah's message with the gentile nations. Although Israel never seeks converts, every Jew is obligated to teach his gentile neighbors[9] how to observe the seven universal laws of morality given to Noah and his descendants.[10]

These efforts are also connected with Redemption. Our Rabbis explain that rewards are given "measure for measure."[11] Since *Mashiach* will perfect the entire world, motivating all the nations to serve G-d together,[12] efforts should be undertaken to encourage all of mankind to refine its conduct.

In these and other ways, Jews have endeavored to prepare the world for Redemption. At present, however, the thrust of these efforts has changed, for the Redemption has become an imminent reality, requiring our people to accept a more radical mission: To make the world conscious of *Mashiach*, and thus steer people's attention to the overriding goal — the purpose for which the world was created.

To explain the concept with an analogy: In the '50s, there was a host of TV programs about Japanese soldiers stranded on remote Pacific islands, unaware that the war was over, waiting to battle the American invaders. No one had bothered to tell them the truth.

In the same way, the spiritual "battle" of previous generations is over. This is reflected in the fact that, as mentioned in earlier chapters, the changes shaping our society have reached

---

9. Maimonides, *Mishneh Torah, Hilchos Melachim* 8:10. See also *Tosafos Yom Tov, Avos* 3:14.
10. These seven laws include the prohibition against the worship of false divinities, blasphemy, murder, incest and adultery, theft, and eating flesh from living animals [and by extension other expressions of cruelty], and the obligation to establish laws and courts of justice. They are discussed by Maimonides (*Loc. cit.,* chs. 9 and 10).
11. *Nedarim* 32a.
12. Maimonides (*Loc. cit.* 11:4).

a scope and intensity that enable us to recognize the backdrop for the Redemption. The world is signaling that it is ready.

So our generation has been granted a new mission: To spread awareness of *Mashiach* and the Redemption, and to make people aware of this new reality.[13]

---

13. See the essay entitled "Open Your Eyes and See" in *Sound the Great Shofar* (Kehot, 1992). (Appendix A.)

CHAPTER 9:

THE BIGGEST QUESTION OF ALL

If we could have an intimate two-way conversation with G-d, one of the first things we would probably ask is: Why did You do it? Why did You create the world?

Philosophers, metaphysicians, and religious leaders have addressed this issue, trying to explain why G-d did what He did. Speaking to Moses on Mount Sinai,[1] G-d answered the question. **Why did G-d create our world? Because He "desired a dwelling in the lower worlds."**[2]

---

1. As conveyed to us by the Oral Tradition.
2. *Midrash Tanchuma, Parshas Bechukosai*, sec. 3.

Well, why did He desire? When one of his followers asked Rabbi Shneur Zalman of Liadi,[3] the Rabbi answered: "When it comes to desire, you don't ask why."

The Rabbi wasn't being flippant. We do plenty of things because we have to, and many because we think they are right. We may not mind doing some of these things and may even enjoy doing others, but we don't desire to do them. When we do something because of desire, we usually don't think about why we desire it: we just desire it, and that's enough.

Often this leads to our doing a lot of silly things. After all, we are speaking of doing things without a reason. But there are times when we desire something and that desire is a response to an inner voice. Something inside is telling us that this is right for us, that it's part of what we must do to really be ourselves.

For example, the Book of Samuel tells us of Chanah's prayer for a child.[4] Chanah had been childless for many years, and came to the Sanctuary at Shiloh, where she "poured out [her] soul before G-d," praying for a son. Her desire flowed from the very depth of her being.

The same can be said of G-d's "desires." When a particular plane of existence is a product of G-d's thought, that plane of existence comes into being. G-d does not, however, share a deep connection with it. When He *desires* something, by contrast, the very essence of His Being is involved.

What does G-d desire from our world? That it be "a dwelling" for Him. G-d created the world, because He wanted a home.

---

3. Founder of the *Chabad* approach to *Chassidic* life.
4. Ch. 1. See the essay entitled "The Inner Motivation for Prayer," *Timeless Patterns in Time* (Kehot, N.Y., 1993), Rosh HaShanah, which develops this concept at length.

A home is where we let loose and are ourselves. We do express ourselves outside our homes as well, but it is not the same. No matter how hard a host tries to make his guests feel comfortable, there are always accepted social conventions, personal reservations, and the like. But when we're at home, it's different. That's where who we really are comes out.[5]

Our world is G-d's home, the place where His essence is expressed. He is the ultimate of good, and it is in our world that this ultimate goodness will be expressed.

Where is the home that G-d desires? To refer to our Sages' expression, "In the lower worlds." This means our material world, not the spiritual realms. In this material world where G-d is only faintly perceived, He will make His home.

When G-d created the world, He left man the task of "building" the house and "furnishing" it so that it becomes fit to serve as a dwelling for Him. Were the world to have been created complete — a G-dly dwelling from the outset — there would have been no concept of "lower worlds." So G-d created a world distinct from Himself — a frame of reference that does not openly appreciate Him, but which can be perfected.[6]

---

5. This concept may be difficult for many Americans to understand, because in our society, the concept of home and family is often misunderstood. But this is a topic for another discussion. See "Doesn't Anyone Ever Blush Anymore" by Manis Friedman (Harper Collins), which touches on these issues.

6. One might ask: Why does G-d's dwelling have to be in the lower worlds? Why can He not express His essence in the spiritual realms?

   For a reply, ask any architect what he is does when he designs a building. He'll tell you that he is seeking to make something new and creative, and simultaneously, functional. These thrusts have their roots in G-d's *designing of His dwelling*, our world.

   Real creativity is rooted in His essence, for it is only He who can create a realm distinct from Him, and in that way, genuinely new. Since G-d's desire expresses His essential self, it follows that it must manifest itself in creation, bringing into being a new frame of reference, one that does not openly appreciate Him.

Fashioning G-d's dwelling in such a world is man's responsibility. In this way, he becomes G-d's partner in creation[7] and earns the most complete form of satisfaction and happiness, the satisfaction that comes from creating and achieving.

Now, it is natural to protest that the world is far from perfect as even a dwelling for man, let alone as a Divine residence. Take a look at what's happening in our inner cities, in the Third World, in Eastern Europe. Is this G-d's dwelling?!

Yes, potentially.

Let's borrow a concept from biology. Gestation refers to the time from conception to birth. Small, uncomplicated forms of life gestate quickly; fruitflies gestate in eleven minutes. As the complexity of the life forms increases, so does the gestation period. For humans, gestation takes nine months.

Ideas also gestate. **The more profound and novel the idea, the longer the gestation period.** When America declared itself a free country, over 20% of its population were slaves. It was almost 100 years before Lincoln freed the slaves, and another 100 before the civil rights movement made that freedom mean something. Ideas take time to take hold.[8]

How long has the world been around? That's about the length of the gestation necessary for it to realize its destiny as G-d's dwelling.

Let's go back to the concept of a home. Our Sages say[9] that "A person who does not have a home is not a person." Unless a person has a home of his own, there is a certain element of his being that will not be fulfilled. Therefore, every person desires

---

7. *Shabbos* 10a.
8. We find a similar concept in Chassidic thought. One of the great *Chassidic* leaders, Rabbi Shlomo of Radomsk said, "It took one moment for G-d to take the Jews out of Egypt, but it took forty years to take Egypt out of the Jews."
9. *Yevamos* 63a and commentary of *Tosafos*; *Sefer HaMaamarim* 5666 p. 520.

a home. But the desire is not necessarily consciously felt. A person can live 30, 40 years or more without realizing that he wants a home.

We must, however, take note of the inner dynamic at work. Our ordinary wants and "needs" seek immediate gratification, but often the focus is only on the immediate. As time passes, our attention shifts to other targets. Genuine, heartfelt desires, by contrast, can wait years to be realized. Since they are part of our inner beings, there is no rush for them to be expressed. Nevertheless, sooner or later, they will definitely surface and become manifest.

The same concept applies regarding G-d's desire to have a dwelling in this world. This desire is not a response to external pressure or stimulation. G-d ingrained it within existence, making it an inner, self-propelling motivation which brought the world into being, and which is constantly shaping its destiny. Just as with man's desire for a home, the timetable of G-d's desire is flexible. The essence of the matter — that our world will become G-d's home — is, by contrast an unchanging truth. Ultimately, it will flourish into complete expression.

Since Redemption will permeate every dimension of existence, every one of us is involved. To illustrate the concept of mutual responsibility, the *Chafetz Chayim* would tell the following parable: Two people were sitting on a ship. One began digging a hole under his seat. When the other protested, the first person replied, "What's it your business? I paid for this seat."

This is only part of the picture. We are not passengers on a cruise; every one of us is part of the crew. Like it or not, everyone plays a role in shaping the future. Already, as our world matures into a global village, it is becoming clear that what each person does affects everyone and everything.[10]

We are all either silent or conscious partners to change. As we take the reins in our hands and focus on the essence of why we are here, we can do our part in enabling G-d's desire for a home in our world to be fulfilled.

---

10. In this vein, contemporary sociologists have stated that Einstein's Theory of Relativity is as true a principle in the realm of social science as it is in physics.

CHAPTER 10:

HORROR AND HOPE;
HOLOCAUST AND REDEMPTION

Some subjects are not pleasant. Failing to take note of them, however, does not make them go away. And therefore, an intellectually honest person is required to confront them. For these reasons, when thinking in terms of the Redemption, although one is tempted to avoid the subject of the Holocaust, the issue cannot be ignored.[1]

---

1. This chapter was originally written out of a commitment to intellectual honesty, a willingness to confront the theoretical issues which arise when thinking of the Redemption. Unfortunately, from time to time, it has become intertwined with current events, for neo-nazism continues to rear its head in Germany and in Europe as a whole.

    It has become a cliché to say that if we don't remember history, we will be forced to relive it. But whether we do or do not remember, our surrounding environment is reminding us that the Holocaust is a possibility that mankind is not horrified by.

Although almost 50 years have passed, for Jews and for that matter, for gentiles, this tragedy still poses a great question in regard to belief in G-d. It is natural to ask: Where was He, and why didn't He do anything to stop it? More particularly, in regard to the Redemption, the question arises: If the Redemption did not come then, when mankind needed it most, when will it come? And others go further, saying that if *Mashiach* didn't come then, they don't want him to come at all. If he was so cruel as to allow that degree of torture and torment to continue, then he is not the leader they want.[2]

To help understand why *Mashiach* did not come then, it is useful to go back in history. When the Romans ruled Israel, they did not have guns and gas chambers, so they could not kill six million at a time, but they also oppressed the Jews severely, and our people yearned for *Mashiach*. The Talmud[3] relates that, at one point during that period, Rabbi Yehoshua ben Levi encountered the prophet Elijah and asked him: "When is *Mashiach* coming?"

Replied the Prophet: "Go and ask him. He's at the gate of Rome."

"How shall I recognize him?"

"He is sitting among paupers stricken by wounds. While the others unbind all their wounds at once, and then bind them up again, he unbinds one wound at a time, and straight away binds

---

2. We have chosen to consider the issue seriously. On the other hand, it must be emphasized that for many, the Holocaust is merely an excuse. They don't want to confront personal change, and are unwilling to accept the apparent sacrifice involved in coming to terms with spiritual values. For them, raising the issue of the Holocaust is a way of saying: "See, I have you stumped, so leave me alone and let me live my life as I please." Such an approach is an affront to the martyrs of the Holocaust, and cheapens the experience which they and mankind underwent.
3. *Sanhedrin* 98a.

it up again. For he says: 'Perhaps I shall be called upon to appear as *Mashiach*, and I must not be delayed!' "

So Rabbi Yehoshua ben Levi went to him and said, "Peace upon you, my master and teacher!"

He answered him, "Peace upon you, son of Levi!"

Then he asked him, "Master, when are you coming?"

He answered, "Today!"

Rabbi Yehoshua returned to Elijah, who asked him, "What did he say?"

Rabbi Yehoshua replied: "He deceived me! He told me, 'I am coming today,' but he has not come!"

Said Elijah: "What *Mashiach* had in mind was this verse: '*today, if you would only listen to His voice!*' "

The Talmud is telling us that **Mashiach wants to come, perhaps even more than mankind wants him to.**[4] Why doesn't he? Because the world is not ready for him.

Could not G-d take care of the problem? Could He not clean up the blotches of evil, strife and injustice that mar our world? Yes, **G-d could, but He wants this task to be fulfilled by man, through "listening to His voice."**

To explain: G-d created our material world because He desired that it become His home.[5] Implicit in this desire is that the dwelling be fashioned by man himself. Thus G-d created a world that was fit to become His dwelling, but only fit. He left

---

4. For "more than the calf wants to suck, the cow wants to give suck" (*Pesachim* 112a).
5. *Midrash Tanchuma, Parshas Bechukosai*, sec. 3, quoted in *Tanya*, ch. 33 and 36. See the explanation of this concept in the previous chapter.

the world — and for that matter, man himself — unfinished, and entrusted the task of putting the finishing touches to this creation to us.[6]

What is man supposed to contribute? An old Chassidic adage says: "G-d made something out of nothing. Man's task is to transform the something into nothing."

The world G-d created is material, and by its nature encourages self-concern — this is the "something" the chassidim mean. What G-d wants from man is to infuse spiritual consciousness into the world, to promote selflessness and personal sacrifice — this is what the chassidim mean when they say man's objective is to transform the something into nothing.

Were these qualities also to have been contributed by G-d, i.e., were He to have made the world a spiritual Garden of Eden, then man would have had little purpose. And were He, at any point in history, to inject these qualities into our lives by bringing the Redemption regardless of man's endeavors, then man's existence would have been an exercise in futility.

Man's purpose is to fashion G-d's dwelling, to create a setting for the Redemption. To enable man to fulfill this purpose, G-d entrusts him with the potential to create, granting him the ability to restructure his environment — both the inner environment of his mind and his external world.[7] Nevertheless, because the contribution expected of man is not entirely defined, and its selfless dimension runs against his nature, it is difficult for him.

For these reasons, the possibility exists that man will misuse his potential. The very energy that could bring Redemption

---

6. Alluding to such a relationship, our Sages (*Shabbos* 119b) state that man has the potential to become G-d's partner in creation.

7. Indeed, we see that man possesses a desire to create and exercising this potential is one of our greatest sources of pleasure and satisfaction.

can lead to holocausts if misdirected. Instead of creating an environment of peace and prosperity, man can use his unique gifts to create hell on earth.

And yet G-d trusts man, and gives him free choice.[8] This — entrusting mankind with his own future — is the most prodigious exercise of Divine generosity and patience possible. For G-d knows what is expected of man, watches him as he succeeds and/or fails, and allows him to continue without interference.

Should there be limits to this trust? I have a friend who is a child psychologist. He tells me that if I see my three-year-old playing with matches, I should not take them away. Instead, I should let the child experience the consequences of his behavior.

The wisdom of this approach is debatable. Whether or not one agrees, the reason he is able to make such a suggestion is obvious; the risks are small. No one would suggest a child be allowed to learn those same lessons when playing with a gun. Guns can kill.

Well, so can holocausts. Still, G-d lets man make them and watches without interfering. Why? How can He?

The question is twofold: a) Mankind can suffer harm, and if G-d is good and wants good, how can He let this harm be inflicted? b) How can He bear watching? We as humans are revolted by cruelty and brutality. Isn't He?

To focus on the first question: An agent of the communist authorities once threatened the Previous Lubavitcher Rebbe, Rabbi Yosef Yitzchak Schneersohn, with a gun, boasting of its power to influence people. The Rebbe replied that a gun can

---

8. See Maimonides, *Mishneh Torah, Hilchos Teshuvah*, chs. 5 and 6, which emphasize the importance of free choice as a fundamental principle of the Jewish faith.

only influence someone who has one world and many gods. "I," he continued, "have one G-d and two worlds."

What the Previous Rebbe was saying is that we have to see the larger picture. When we conceive of life as being limited to the immediate here and now of bodily existence, then death is terrifying. When we are aware of spiritual reality, and have faith in an afterlife, reincarnation, and resurrection, physical death becomes just another milestone in life.

Rav Aryeh Levine used to say that when a baby is born, everyone laughs, but the baby cries. When a person dies, by contrast, everyone cries; perhaps the soul is laughing?

When seen in an overall perspective, it is clear that loss is not felt by those who die, but only by those who remain; the suffering experienced on this plane — awesome and extreme as it can be — is fleeting in nature. What is important in our lives is the lasting contributions we make. In that context, the legacy of martyrdom and the sanctification of both life and death which the victims of the Holocaust left us looms colossal on our spiritual horizons.

In regard to the second question: How can G-d bear the pain suffered by His children? The answer is simple. He can't. Therefore, to cite the Bible's expression,[9] He "hides His face."

But He allows the suffering to continue. Why? Because as difficult as it is for Him to bear man's suffering, it is even more difficult to take back the gift of free will which He has given us. He refuses to condemn man to the status of a robot. G-d wants man to be a creator, and to use that potential to fashion a G-dly dwelling in our material world.

---

9.   *Deuteronomy* 31:17; see the commentary of *Baalei Tosafos*.
      This expression also contains an allusion. The Hebrew word for "face," *ponim*, also means "inner dimension." When G-d hides His face, His inner dimensions are still being expressed; they are, however, working in a hidden way.

We cannot explain the Holocaust. Indeed, any explanation or rationale seems vulgar and crass. Observations, however, can be made; and one thing is clear. Holocausts do not happen every day, or for that matter, every century. The awesomeness of the tragedy and its effect — the utter collapse of the Jewish life that had nourished our people for centuries — points to a transition of prodigious scope.[10]

Throughout our people's history, there have been miracles, e.g., the exodus from Egypt or the Maccabees' defeat of the Greeks, which inaugurated change. The Holocaust was, by contrast, an anti-miracle, but it too was symptomatic of a monumental change.

At that time, all the major Sages described that era as *Ikvesa diMeshicha* — **the time when Mashiach's approaching footsteps can be heard.** But as we stated above, G-d made *Mashiach's* coming dependent on man. For *Mashiach* to come, radical change is necessary in the world at large. Man has the capacity to cause such a change, and to cause it to be positive. But when a potential exists, it is also possible for the pendulum to swing in the opposite direction.

Our Sages knew about these dangers. One of them said: "Let him [*Mashiach*] come, but let me not see his coming."[11] He wanted the Redemption to take place, but sought to be spared the anguish that might precede its coming.

---

10. Another one of the observations forced upon us by the Holocaust is an awareness of the Jews' uniqueness as a people. It is nice to think in universal terms and to speak about mankind as a whole. But Hitler's universalism was limited. Although he killed people of all nationalities, the full force of his death machine was directed against the Jews. And the other nations did not protest, or lift a finger to stop him. To quote the title of a best-selling book, "The Jews Were Expendable."

11. *Sanhedrin* 98b.

Our Prophets[12] speak of the Redemption as being preceded by birthpangs. Ask any woman who has given birth, and she'll tell you that however great the pain, the start of a new life remains the most powerful dimension of the experience. And the most lasting.

The *Kabbalah* explains that every fundamental process of transition has three phases: *yesh* — *ayin* — *yesh*, an entity, a state of void, and a new entity. For when one wants to take a radical step forward, one must first negate the previous frame of reference.[13] Then, like a vacuum, this state of non-being "draws in" a new and higher level of existence. The metamorphosis from the old world of the *shtetl* (in Jewish terms) and the formative years of the Industrial Revolution (in terms of the world at large) to the Era of the Redemption needed an *ayin*.

As mankind was groping for a formula for change, Hitler offered his definition of *ayin* — absolute annihilation. In the half-century that has followed, mankind has begun to seek more positive definitions, ones that further G-d's purpose in Creation. And this will enable us not merely to hear the footsteps of *Mashiach*, but to see his coming and share in the era of fulfillment he will initiate.

---

12. See *Hosea* 13:13, *Isaiah* 37:3, 66:8.
13. To illustrate this principle: After making *aliyah* to *Eretz Yisrael*, Rabbi Zeira undertook one hundred fasts in order to *forget* the Babylonian Talmud, so that he would be able to appreciate the different thinking processes underlying the Jerusalem Talmud (B. *Metzia* 85a).

CHAPTER 11:

A PARADIGM FOR LEADERSHIP

At some point in our lives, many of us have shared a relationship with a parent, teacher, or employer which deeply affected us. That person had high standards. He stood for something and invited others to stand with him.

He was demanding; he never gave in and never accepted mediocre performance. But he also never gave up, and constantly communicated high expectations and the trust that we could meet them.

Such trust and confidence empower us. When we look up to someone with well-earned respect and feel that he genuinely knows us and believes in us, it is natural to want to live up to his expectations. With a pride that goes much deeper than self, we apply ourselves to the tasks before us, for our goal is not merely to earn reward, but to give shape and form to the ideal we share.

What would happen — and with modern communications this is a possibility — if a leader of this nature were to arise and to reach out to all mankind?

This is what the coming of *Mashiach* will be like.

The concept of *Mashiach* is hard for modern man to accept. We no longer have kings, and even charismatic leaders are few and far between. Our institutions have moved toward decentralization, but even these smaller systems need leaders in order to function effectively.

The scarcity of genuine leadership is a source of concern in politics, business and culture. Analysts have complained that America is over-managed and under-led. They indict the individuals at the heads of our organizations for being far too concerned with the bottom line, for trying to maintain a structure that produces a favorable annual report, instead of desiring to inspire creative change.

True leadership requires vision. People can be forced into following, but even while that control is enforced, negative feelings will be aroused, for humans have a natural tendency to resist coercion.

Similarly, compliance can be obtained through exchange. Goods and services can be bartered for conformity. Many of the relationships in our homes and workplaces operate because bargains of this nature are constantly being made.

When leadership which promises rewards of this nature is exercised fairly, it can be functional and satisfying. Nevertheless, such a system encourages selfishness rather than idealism and teamwork, for the basic motivator is the person's own benefit, the payoff.[1] Nor will this form of leadership inspire true growth. For a person barters for what he perceives is good, and thus can never advance beyond the level of his immediate understanding.

Genuine leadership must inspire people with a longterm vision that gives meaning to their efforts. It must point them in a new direction, endow them with deeper understanding and higher aspirations, and show how their actions form an indispensable part of a purposeful whole.

It is important to emphasize the difference between inspiration and demagoguery. A demagogue can get people excited, but he speaks about unrealistic expectations.[2] The vision with which a genuine leader inspires others, by contrast, rings true.

Like an idea which makes a listener say: "Aha! I always understood that, but never had words for it," a leader's vision touches a chord within the inner self of others. The framework which a leader offers is unique and different, enlarging his followers' horizons, but is nevertheless something plainly possible — a goal with which others can identify.

Mashiach will share such an ideal with all mankind. *Mashiach's* dream is to make our world a dwelling for G-d. On one hand, this vision is unique and radical, for it requires an understanding of existence far different than that found in our ordinary approach to life. On the other hand, this vision can be appreciated by everyone; indeed, it relates to every dimension

---

1.   In a related context, our Sages (*Pirkei Avos* 5:10) state: "[Saying] 'what's mine is mine and what's yours is yours'... is characteristic of the people of Sodom." For the line between legitimate self-interest and selfishness is a fine one, and can be distinguished only by the guiding light of true values.

2.   And often, there is a negative twist to the message of a demagogue: The ideal is not being realized because some people — or some traits in one's personality — are preventing it from being realized. And much of the focus goes into combating these opposing forces.

of existence. For this is the intent which motivated the very creation of the world.[3]

And this message echoes within the heart of each of us. We would all like to live in security and abundance, with a chance to develop our potential to its fullest.

The factors enabling the expression of these values are already at work. The forces of change within our society are sweeping away the old systems and dogmas, and have created systems that enable us to anticipate the ideals of peace, wisdom, and unity that will characterize the Redemption.

Nevertheless, if the backdrop for Redemption is in the process of being created, it is only a backdrop; in the foreground, the newspapers are still filled with violence, poverty, and war. Our technology has advanced more quickly than we have, and until we attain more wisdom, sensitivity and truth, the dream of the Redemption will not be realized.

What is going to make the difference? How will we translate our aspirations from the abstract to the practical?

For change to be purposeful rather than random, it must be brought about by people sharing ideals and principles with others. This leads to one of Judaism's fundamental concepts: that the Era of the Redemption is not merely an age of awareness and peace, it is *Yemos HaMashiach*, "the days of *Mashiach*."[4]

---

3. *Midrash Tanchuma, Parshas Bechukosai*, sec. 3.
4. *Sanhedrin* 99a discusses the proposition that the Redemption will not be led by a mortal. Instead, "the Holy One, blessed be He, will rule Himself; He will redeem them." The Talmud, however, rejects this thesis, repudiating it to the extent that the *Chasam Sofer* (*Yoreh Deah*, Responsum 356) states that a person who subscribes to this notion "denies the entire Torah."

Mashiach's teachings will inspire a series of real changes in our approach to life.[5] As people throughout the world become aware of his message, they will desire to take part in spreading the atmosphere of spiritual purpose, knowledge and peace. This will create a bridge between the ideal and the actual, allowing mankind to create an environment appropriate for a world that is G-d's dwelling.

This ideal is fundamental to Judaism's concept of Redemption. For Judaism sees the coming of the Redemption as dependent on the growth and spread of human wisdom. *Mashiach* will not descend from heaven. He will be a human being who will teach others to be more human, and to be more than human by expressing the G-dly potential we all possess.

There is no alternative. There is no way that we can develop a perfect society without perfecting people; we must refine our characters. And it will be a flesh and blood human being, *Mashiach*, whose personal example and leadership will inspire others to make such changes — within themselves, and then within their environment.

When people are dedicated to realizing an ideal, they rise above petty self-concern. They appreciate what another person can contribute, and are eager to accept his input. Such an approach has a tremendous binding power, for there is no bond more potent than a shared ideal.

For a leader's vision to be communicated effectively, it must be reflected in his personal life. Trust is a follower's response to a leader's vision. And we will not trust — nor entrust our energies to — a leader unless he embodies the principles he espouses. People must see personal integrity, consistency, and genuine sincerity in a leader before they will consent to follow.

---

5.   See Maimonides, *Mishneh Torah, Hilchos Teshuvah* 9:2.

For that reason, not only will *Mashiach* reveal how the world at large is G-d's dwelling, but this concept will be realized in his own person. The spark of G-d — the soul which is present in all men — will burn brightly in him, dominating his personality; "The spirit of G-d will rest upon him, the spirit of wisdom and understanding, the spirit of counsel and strength, the spirit of knowledge and fear of G-d."[6]

The necessity for *Mashiach* to serve as an example of realized human potential is reflected in the criteria which Maimonides provides for recognizing a potential Redeemer.[7] First, he states that *Mashiach* must be a descendant of the House of David; i.e., he will be heir to the virtues that distinguish the Jewish monarch. Furthermore, *Mashiach* will be a Torah sage of deep understanding, whose conduct reflects the spiritual truths he has uncovered.

The next criterion mentioned by Maimonides — that *Mashiach* will inspire the entire Jewish people to a deeper commitment to their Jewish heritage — reflects another important dimension of leadership: A leader cannot be a visionary in the wilderness. He must be a successful communicator, a person who gets his message across, and who makes his followers understand that he appreciates them and their role in shaping the shared vision. This stirs a wholehearted, uninhibited, and dynamic commitment on their part.

This leads to a further point. A leader's vision must translate ideals into applicable principles. Although *Mashiach* will be a teacher *par excellence*, communicating wisdom to all people, his intent will not be to impart abstract knowledge, but to bring about actual change throughout the world. As Maimon-

---

6. *Isaiah* 11:2.
7. *Mishneh Torah, Hilchos Melachim* 11:4. See also the explanation of these criteria in the essay entitled "The Function of *Mashiach*" in *I Await His Coming* (Kehot, 1991).

ides continues:[8] "*Mashiach* will... perfect the entire world, [motivating all the nations] to serve G-d together."

---

8.   *Op. cit.*

CHAPTER 12:

WILL MASHIACH WORK MIRACLES?

Our previous chapter described *Mashiach* as a teacher and leader. Is that all? What about the miracles he will perform?

First, let's see what we mean by a miracle. The *Book of Kings*[1] tells us the following story: Idolatry was rampant in Israel and therefore, the land was plagued by drought. Elijah the prophet appeared before Ahab, the idol-worshipping king, and told him to prepare a confrontation between himself and the prophets of Baal.

Both he and the heathen prophets would build altars on Mount Carmel. They would both sacrifice bulls, but would not kindle fire under the sacrifices. The power that would send fire from heaven to consume the sacrifice would be accepted as

---

1. *I Kings*, ch. 18.

G-d. The prophets of Baal offered their sacrifice first, and called out to their god fervently, but there was no answer.

Elijah then built an altar to G-d, offered his sacrifice, had it doused with water (to prove the miracle was not a ruse), and then called upon G-d. And He answered, sending down a great flame which consumed the sacrifice, the altar, and the water.

Most people associate the coming of Mashiach with wonders of this nature, and think of Mashiach as a miracle-worker. On one hand, the image is attractive. Everyone enjoys seeing the amazing, particularly if these miracles are to their benefit.

On the other hand, the very notion of miracles is strange, even threatening to some of us. For miracles require the adoption of a new world view, and we are not excited about doing that. We would like tomorrow to go on more or less like yesterday without ruffling the routines of our everyday lives. Miracles surely upset these norms, and that makes us uneasy.

Theoretically, the concept of Mashiach as a miracle worker raises three questions: a) Do miracles take place? b) Can miracles happen in the present age? c) Is there a connection between miracles and Mashiach's coming?

a) Do miracles happen?

We all tell our children stories of the ten plagues in Egypt, and of the cruse of oil which burnt for eight days on Chanukah, but often people tell these stories like fairy tales. They have a hard time accepting that these things actually took place. And because they tell the stories this way, it's no wonder that when they grow up, their children also have a hard time believing them.

This is a fundamental issue. Believing that there is a G-d above nature, and that He can make miracles happen as He desires is not escapism. It is an appreciation of the true reality. G-d created the world and brought into being the natural order from absolute nothingness. In doing so, He established a pattern which governs our existence, but not His.

The moment-to-moment working of the natural order is also G-d's doing. Indeed, nature can be considered a continuous series of miracles,[2] since everything, even the fluttering of a leaf in the wind, occurs due to Divine Providence.[3] Since He maintains the natural order as an exercise of His will, He can intervene in the workings of our world whenever He desires.

b) Can miracles happen in the present age?

Even if we admit that miracles happen, it's far more comfortable to consider them as past history. Miracles in the past don't present a personal challenge. It is a very different story to say miracles can affect our lives today.

Jewish law[4] requires that a person who sees a place where a miracle occurred recite a blessing: "Blessed are You, G-d, our L-rd, King of the universe, who wrought a miracle for me in this place."

After the rescue of Israel's hostages in Entebbe (1976), one of them asked Rabbi Moshe Feinstein, the leading *halachic* authority of the time, whether he would be required to recite this blessing if he ever visited Entebbe again. Rabbi Feinstein said yes.[5]

---

2. Responsa of *Chacham Tzvi* 18; *Kesser Shem Tov* sec. 256.
3. Rabbi Israel Baal Shem Tov as quoted in *Kesser Shem Tov, Hosafos,* sec. 119ff. See the essay entitled "Masterplan The Baal Shem Tov's Unique Conception of Divine Providence" (Sichos In English, 5752).
4. *Maimonides, Mishneh Torah, Hilchos Berachos* 10:9; *Shulchan Aruch, Orach Chayim* 218:9.
5. See *HaPardes,* Tammuz 5739.

And on a global scale, the collapse of the Iron Curtain and the crumbling of communism, the events of the Gulf War, and the arrival of massive waves of immigrants to *Eretz Yisrael* are events whose miraculous nature stands out boldly. Yes, there could be a natural explanation for all these occurrences. But you could also give a natural explanation for the splitting of the Red Sea (there was, after all, an east wind blowing throughout the night). The fact is that if a person had predicted the events of recent years a decade ago, his statements would have been considered preposterous. Ask any soldier who served in the Gulf; he'll tell you that miracles are just as possible today as they were in the past.

c) Is there a connection between miracles and Mashiach's coming?

This is a question concerning which there is a difference of opinion among our Sages. Our prophets say:[6] "As in the days of your exodus from Egypt, I will show you wonders," implying that the exodus from Egypt serves as the archetype for redemption, and that the future Redemption will also be characterized by great miracles. Similarly, we find many prophecies of *Mashiach's* coming, e.g., "a wolf will dwell with the lamb,"[7] which clearly point to a fundamental change in the natural order.

In the Talmud,[8] however, there is a difference of opinion about the matter. Rabbi Chiya bar Abba says the prophets' words are to be understood literally and the Era of the Redemption will be characterized by miracles. Another Sage, Shmuel, differs, stating: "There is no difference between the

---

6. *Michah* 7:15. See the booklet entitled "I Will Show You Wonders" (Sichos In English, 1991), which associates this verse with miracles that occurred during the Jewish year 5751 (1991-1992), and explains that they served as a harbinger of Redemption.

7. *Isaiah* 11:6.

8. *Berachos* 34b.

current age and the Era of *Mashiach* except the subjugation [of Israel] to the [gentile] kingdoms."

According to this view, as explained by Maimonides,[9] the prophets' statements are merely allegories used to describe the changes that will occur at that time. For example, in the prophecy cited above, the "wolf" represents the gentile nations, and the "lamb" the Jewish people; in the Era of the Redemption, the Jews will live at peace with the gentiles. Similarly, in regard to the Era of Redemption as a whole: its advent will bring about a transition in every phase of our lives. Nevertheless, the natural order will not be upset.

Maimonides makes similar statements regarding *Mashiach* as an individual:[10]

> One should not entertain the notion that the King *Mashiach* must work miracles and wonders, bring about new phenomena within the world, resurrect the dead, or perform other similar deeds. This is [definitely] not true.
>
> A proof can be brought from the fact that Rabbi Akiva, one of the greatest Sages of the *Mishnah*, supported King Ben Koziva,[11] and would describe him as the King *Mashiach*.... The Sages did not ask him for any signs or wonders.

---

9. *Mishneh Torah, Hilchos Melachim* 12:1.
10. *Ibid.,* 11:3.
11. Bar Kochba. Rabbi Akiva's support of Bar Kochba is significant in another context. The fact that Rabbi Akiva applied the title *Mashiach* to Bar Kochba although he had not yet liberated Israel from the Romans or rebuilt the Temple indicates that a person can be called *Mashiach* although the Redemption is not yet a *fait accompli*. Similarly, in subsequent generations, our nation's Torah leaders have looked to particular individuals as having the potential to be *Mashiach*. See *Sanhedrin* 98b and *Sound the Great Shofar* (Kehot, 1992), pgs. 21-22, 107-108.

Maimonides continues,[12] focusing on "the main thrust of the matter: This Torah, with its statutes and laws, is everlasting"; i.e., his conception of *Mashiach* is that of a Torah leader, not a miracle worker.

There are other Rabbis[13] who advance the opinion that the Era of the Redemption will be characterized by miracles. Similarly, in regard to *Mashiach*, they posit that he will prove his identity by performing wonders. Significantly, in another text,[14] Maimonides himself mentions the possibility of *Mashiach* coming in a miraculous manner.

In subsequent generations, the Rabbis[15] have tried to resolve these two views, explaining that Maimonides also believes there will come a time when the natural order will give way to a miraculous frame of reference. For Maimonides lists as the last of his Thirteen Principles of Faith,[16] belief in the Resurrection of the Dead; this surely represents a drastic deviation from the natural order.

Thus these authorities explain that, according to Maimonides, there will be two periods in the Era of the Redemption: one directly following the coming of *Mashiach* in which the current natural order will continue to prevail, and a subsequent period of miraculous occurrences, including the Resurrection of the Dead.

From a philosophic perspective, we can appreciate the necessity for two periods. In the Era of the Redemption it will

---

12. *Loc. cit.*
13. See the gloss of the *Ra'avad* to the *Mishneh Torah*.
14. *Iggeres Taiman.*
15. *Likkutei Sichos*, Vol. 27, p. 198 ff; see the essay entitled "Two Periods Within the Era of the Redemption" in *I Await His Coming* (Kehot, 1991).
16. *Commentary to the Mishnah*, Introduction to the tenth chapter of the tractate of *Sanhedrin*. The shortened, popular form of these Thirteen Principles (in which each begins *Ani Ma'amin*) is included at the conclusion of the morning service in many *Siddurim*.

be revealed that our world is a dwelling for G-d.[17] Were it necessary for the Era of the Redemption to involve miracles, this would seem to imply that the world as it exists in its present form could not, Heaven forbid, serve as such a dwelling. It would thus appear that the natural order stands in opposition to the manifestation of His presence. Therefore the Era of the Redemption will include a period when the natural order remains and yet, "the occupation of the entire world will be solely to know G-d."[18]

In this framework, *Mashiach's* goal will be to initiate a new age of understanding and knowledge. To do this, he will be a teacher and leader. The wonders he works must be within people's minds, not necessarily within the world at large.

The concept of the world as G-d's dwelling, however, leads to a further concept. Just as a person expresses himself freely in his own home, G-d's essence will be revealed within our material world. This implies the revelation, not only of the limited dimensions of G-dliness that can be enclothed within the confines of the natural order, but also the expression of transcendent aspects of G-dliness whose manifestation will nullify that natural order. These transcendent qualities will be revealed in the second period of the Era of the Redemption.[19]

---

17. See *Likkutei Sichos*, Vol. XII, *Parshas Tazria*, p. 73 ff.
18. Maimonides, *Mishneh Torah*, loc. cit. 12:5.
19. There is, nevertheless, the possibility that even the initial phases of *Mashiach's* coming will be accompanied by miracles. We are referring to the following Talmudic concept (*Sanhedrin* 98a):

    It is written (*Daniel* 7:13), "Behold, one like a son of man came on the clouds of heaven"; however, it is also written (*Zechariah* 9:9), "[Your king will come...] like a poor man riding on a donkey." If [mankind is found worthy,] he will come "on the clouds of heaven." If we are not found worthy, he will come "like a poor man riding on a donkey."

    Thus man's virtue, or lack of it, will determine whether *Mashiach* will come in a transcendent, miraculous manner or will follow the slow, but steady path of a donkey's progress.

CHAPTER 13:

KINGSHIP IN CONTEMPORARY SOCIETY

We are fascinated by monarchy. Although years have passed, the royal wedding in England and the imperial funeral in Tokyo still rank among the all-time media events. On the other hand, humanity has chosen other forms of government, and in a functional sense, the institution of monarchy no longer exists.

The Torah teaches that *Mashiach* will be a king, restoring the dynasty of his ancestor David. This concept presents a challenge for modern man. Even an individual who is able to think of the Redemption as an imminent reality, and who appreciates that it will be *Mashiach* whose teachings will initiate this age of knowledge and peace, may gulp at the idea of serving a king.

The existence of a king — an absolute monarch, not merely a ceremonial figurehead — is foreign to our world view. Our difficulty has to do not so much with the fact that in a functional sense monarchy has ceased to exist, but with the fundamental concept at the heart of a subject-king relationship. We are not willing to subjugate our lives to another human being. On the contrary, democracy and the concept of rule by consent have become accepted as absolute values by most developed cultures and societies.

What is the motivating principle for this consensus? Fundamentally, a commitment to the principle of equality — that all men are created equal and deserve equal rights.

The expression of this ideal in contemporary society is, moreover, a pragmatic one. It is understood that if the ideals of democracy were followed to extremes and a referendum were taken before every step by a government, society could not function. The current compromise — representative democracy — still allows individuals a direct role in determining the future of the society in which they live, yet keeps leaders responsible to the populace.

There is, however, an inherent difficulty with democracies. Their essential motivator is enlightened self-interest; in essence, people are saying to each other, "Let us build a culture that will allow us all to be happy." This approach often accentuates the lowest common denominator, ultimately stripping people of the prideful self-worth that leads to purpose-oriented growth. This is not a necessary byproduct of the democratic ideal, but in actual life, people often fail to live up to their ideals. Lacking genuine inspiration, democratic societies often suffer from a vacuum of direction, which causes time, principles, and values to be sacrificed to enable a host of petty desires to be fulfilled. Slowly, the drive for meaningful achievement and excellence is eroded.

This has been the fate of earlier democracies. We have seen periods of growth and success, but once that success is achieved, each such country has grown fat and declined. This happened to England in the early part of the century. America is grappling with such a downswing at present. And to all appearances, such a cycle is already at work in Japan, for the microchip has accelerated not only the speed of information transfer, but also that of cultural development and decline.

Is there an alternative? The Torah[1] states that Israel should be ruled by a king. In his *Mishneh Torah*,[2] Maimonides describes the appointment of a king as a *mitzvah*, and states[3] that kingship within Israel is not merely a temporary phenomenon, but rather was granted to David and his descendants forever. Continuing in this vein, he describes the Messianic ideal as centering around the person of a king, *Mashiach*, who will renew the Davidic dynasty.[4]

This is not because democracy was unknown in his time. On the contrary, Maimonides was well-versed in Greek philosophy, and was aware of the concept. He extols the virtues of monarchy because this is the Torah's ideal.

From the Torah's perspective, mankind's rejection of monarchy has been due to the failure of kings, and not to the failure of kingship. As humanity as a whole progressed, kings who did not live up to their office could no longer command obedience. But these were the faults of the individuals, not of the institution.

Monarchy is not only a viable system, it is a preferable system — provided the king fulfills the role outlined by Maimon-

---

1. *Deuteronomy* 17:15.
2. *Hilchos Melachim* 1:1.
3. *Op. cit.* 1:8-9.
4. *Loc. cit.* 11:1.

ides for a Jewish monarch:[5] "In all matters, his deeds shall be for the sake of Heaven. His purpose and intent shall be to elevate mankind's faith, and to fill the world with justice."

Though a radical notion, we who have experienced democratic society can also appreciate the primacy of such a form of monarchy. A desire for short-term satisfaction rather than long-term growth and purpose plagues most democracies. It can be overcome only by inspired leadership. What sort of leader would this be? One who has no desire to show authority, no fear of being unpopular, no immediate desire to be loved, and who shows selfless devotion to his people.

What are the chances that such a leader could emerge in a democratic system? Quite low. It's true that in developed democracies, the rise of a leader who flaunts his authority and desires coercive control is a virtual impossibility. But how many people who do not fear becoming unpopular and who do not seek the immediate approval of their constituency will be elected, and reelected? And with all due respect to our politicians, in a society whose fundamental motivator is self-concern, selfless devotion to others is a rare commodity.

In pointing to the need for leadership in the business world, it has been said: Managers are people who do things right, leaders are people who do right things. This also applies in the realm of human relations and social dynamics.

The primary elements of leadership are vision and value-oriented purpose. A leader must introduce a perspective which inspires his followers and motivates them to purposeful growth. There are inherent obstacles to doing this in a democratic society. For doing the right thing often involves a measure of personal sacrifice, at least at the beginning. How easy would it be for an elected leader to convince people to follow his plan if

---

5.   *Loc. cit.* 4:10.

doing so involves giving up opportunities for immediate success and satisfaction?[6]

Moreover, right and wrong are rarely black and white in today's world. To chart a path for his people in the gray areas, a leader requires a mandate of trust that is not dependent on their fickle whims.

Plainly put, the less a leader needs to worry about what his people think of him, the more he can devote himself to promoting their true welfare. If he is constantly in need of their approval, he will be sorely tempted to win that approval by playing "election politics," catering to their desire for immediate satisfaction rather than dedicating himself to their ultimate wellbeing. Only a leader who does not have to worry about the strength of his position can focus his attention on the true nature of his people and seek to develop their potential over the long term.

Ideally, giving a leader a position of established authority should not bring him to divorce himself from his people's thoughts. On the contrary, successful leadership depends on the constant identification of a people with its leader, a continual sharing of a sense of purpose. He must communicate with them, for the most effective means of encouraging a following is not by force or bribery, but by inspiration. Nevertheless, to establish a basis for this communication a leader must have — in addition to his own resources of inner strength and purpose — a secure position of strength and power.

Is not monarchy a more proficient system than democracy for cultivating such leadership? Would not the strength of a king's position make it possible for him to dedicate himself to

---

6. Ultimately, doing what's right will also benefit every individual, but that involves taking a long-term perspective. Unfortunately, however, most of us have a tendency to look at the short-term, and in regard to short-term results, doing what's right often involves sacrifice.

others more effectively than if he were required to go out and win their votes time and again?[7]

Another virtue of monarchy is the dynamic of empowerment that lies at its heart. Monarchy depends on the whole-hearted, uninhibited commitment of the subject to the king, a commitment made knowingly and thoughtfully, not on the basis of blind faith or witless obedience. Ideally, this will awaken a similar commitment on the part of the king, motivating him to dedicate himself to the welfare of his subjects without thought of personal concern.

At a given point in our lives, most of us have experienced a parallel to such a relationship. We have looked up to a parent, a teacher or an employer for much more than what was demanded by the terms of our implicit social contract. We saw them as a source of inner strength and meaningful direction, and put our trust in them, inviting their authority. And this enabled them to impart strength to us; their example and commitment empowered us to develop our own hidden resources.[8]

In a similar vein, our Sages taught:[9] "The servant of a king is like a king." For by making a willful commitment to a king, a person steps beyond the petty concerns of his ego, and this

---

7. A parallel can be seen in the business world. Japanese society is known to be far less open and more accustomed to hierarchical authority than American society. Nevertheless, it is the heads of American business who are accused of being oligarchic and of "looking out for Number 1," while the Japanese are praised for their awareness that in order for the captain of a ship to prosper, the status of the entire crew and all its passengers must also be improved.
8. Some may look at the development of such relationships as a blend of youthful idealism and hero-worship, appropriate perhaps in the formative stages of our development, but not becoming for adults. See the chapter, "A Child Shall Lead Them," which explains the advantage of maintaining certain childlike traits throughout life.
9. *Shavuos* 47b.

opens him to the inner strength and purpose which the king radiates.

It can be argued that these advantages may be true in theory, but the institution of monarchy has not functioned according to these ideals. Throughout history, kings have shown themselves to be no more refined than mankind as a whole.[10] Indeed, this is the main reason societies have, at great sacrifice, chosen democracy. For the right to choose our leader is a safeguard against being manipulated by an unjust, self-serving monarch. By holding a leader accountable to his people, we make sure that he shows concern for their interests as well as for his own.

Such a check against the abuse of power will not be necessary in regard to *Mashiach* for two reasons: a) *Mashiach* will represent the ultimate in personal refinement. He will be a Torah sage whose sole concern will be for the improvement of mankind as a whole.[11] b) *Mashiach* is charged with a mission, to improve the world at large and usher in an age of knowledge and peace. This mission can be fulfilled only with G-d's help. Were *Mashiach* to abuse the authority he is granted, he would not receive G-d's assistance.

Earthly monarchy stems from and serves as an analogy to our relationship with the King of kings. The purpose of a Jewish monarch is to teach the people self-nullification to the king in order to heighten their feelings of self-nullification to G-d.[12] Thus the reinstitution of the monarchy by *Mashiach* will

---

10. See also *I Samuel*, ch. 10, where the prophet warns the people against kingship. Our Sages (*Sanhedrin* 20b) and our Rabbis (Maimonides, *Mishneh Torah, Hilchos Melachim* 1:2) explain that Samuel's statements do not represent a rejection of kingship (for he subsequently appointed a king), but an emphasis on the manner in which a king and a people should approach the institution.
11. Maimonides, *op. cit.* 11:4.
12. *Derech Mitzvosecha, Mitzvas Minui Melech*. See the essay entitled "From Sinai to Mashiach" in *Timeless Patterns of Time* (Kehot, N.Y., 1993), where this concept is explained in depth.

ultimately lead to the fulfillment of the prophecy:[13] "G-d will be King over the entire earth. On that day, G-d shall be One and His name One."

---

13. *Zechariah* 14:9.

CHAPTER 14:

THE FUTURE IN THE PRESENT

One of the great poets and philosophers of medieval Spain, Rabbi Avraham Ibn Ezra, would say: "The past no longer exists; the future is not yet a reality; the present is but a fleeting moment. Why then should one worry?"[1]

The first three clauses of his statement are very true in the present time. Clearly, "the past no longer exists." To cite some obvious examples: The types of jobs which built our society for the past half-century or more are no longer viable alternatives for those entering the labor force today. In geopolitics, the fall of the Communist bloc has mandated a rethinking of the positions that have dominated national policies since the Second World War. Even the place in which we live is often no longer

---

1.   The Hebrew original, ‏העבר אין, העתיד עדיין, ההוה כהרף עין. דאגה מנין?‏, has rhyme and rhythm which is unfortunately lacking in translation.

the same, for there has been a mass exodus from the industrial northeast to the sunbelt, and within both these regions, mobility is the norm.

"The future is not yet a reality." That is also plainly true; for although we see changes on the horizon — among them, the proliferation of robots in our factories, revolutions in nutrition and health, and a shifting of power from national to local governments — it will take time before the impact of these changes is fully felt.

"The present is but a fleeting moment." And its fleeting nature is certainly felt today, when innovations in travel and communications have accelerated the rate of change beyond all expectations.

But the last clause of Rabbi Ibn Ezra's statement: "Why then should one worry?" is another matter. Within many spheres of society, there is worry. During a transition, people question themselves and their situation, and search for understanding. As they wrestle with an uncertain present and an unknown future, it is natural for them to cling to the past instead of embracing the future.

And the challenge is more difficult than ever because the future is exploding with diversity. Rather than either-or choices, we are presented with multiple options which force us to apply ourselves to the process of decision-making with far more thought than impulse.

We cannot afford to tread water, for the current is moving forward, and if we do not move with it, we lose the opportunity to determine our destiny. When seen in such a light, an awareness of the present is an arrow pointing to the future. For what tomorrow will be is very much a result of what today is.

Once the newly appointed dean of a university was asked to try to prevail upon the students to stop walking on the grass between the library and the student union.

"Why do they walk on the grass?" the dean asked.

"Because it is the most direct route between the two buildings," his associates answered.

"Then cut a path through the grass," the dean responded.

In other words, it is useless to try to hinder the inevitable. Instead, one should try to understand the reasons for the changes and seek to find the most appropriate response.

From a Jewish perspective, the changes in our society are symptomatic of a transition of a more encompassing nature. We are on the threshold of the Era of Redemption, and indeed, in the process of crossing that threshold. In that context, the changes occurring throughout our society can be seen as creating the backdrop for this era of peace, prosperity, and wisdom. For example, two of the most important trends in contemporary economics — the existence of a global village and the reduction of the labor force (painful as it is) — can be interpreted as a foretaste of world unity and peace, and the potential for man to devote his energies to personal and spiritual growth rather than to earning his livelihood. Similarly, as mentioned in several previous chapters, in many other ways the physical setting for the Redemption is within our grasp; all that is lacking is the spiritual knowledge that will be revealed by *Mashiach*.

Moreover, the nature of these changes is creating an openness for such spiritual knowledge. We are moving from an industrial to an information society, and this creates a demand for intellectual creativity. And here, there is a connection to the spiritual, because the mind has the capacity to reach upward, and to seek for depth and meaning above the grasp of intellect alone.

Furthermore, exposure to an avalanche of technology has created a need for spiritual balance. As we are forced to process vast amounts of information every day and do so at a far greater speed than ever before, we feel a desire to balance this element of our lives with a spiritual dimension.

Throughout America and the world at large, people are genuinely searching for spiritual meaning. They want to be more in touch with themselves, with other people, and with nature, and to appreciate the inner spiritual core that binds them together.

This spiritual quest is not otherworldly. The motivation is not to lift oneself into a realm of spiritual consciousness and forget one's ordinary experience, but rather to permeate one's ordinary experience with understanding and purpose. In one sense, people are far less idealistic than in the '60s. Then youth were willing to give up everything, and now they want the comforts of middle-class America. On the other hand, today's spiritual aspirations are much more realistic, and there is a greater potential for integrating these desires within our daily lives.

And this points to another important trend. Although in the realm of communications and economics, the global village is a reality, when it comes down to day-to-day living, everyone is far more concerned with what is happening in his own back-yard. The fact that we can reach the world has caused us to wear mental bifocals, and to narrow as well as to expand our horizons. Before it was possible to have an effect on the world at large, our energy was to a large extent directed outward. As the scope within which we can effect change has grown, we have learned the need for inwardness.

In searching for the appropriate response, many people have adopted a positive selfishness, i.e., a commitment to inner change and personal growth. Instead of blaming others, they realize that they must take responsibility for their lives, and are endeavoring to do so.

Nor is this thrust self-contained. Family has taken on new importance, as people seek to share with their children and develop meaningful relationships. And the process of developing meaningful relationships has, in many sectors, spread into the workplace, as communication skills have become recognized as an important business commodity.

This setting is appropriate to the spiritual purpose of Redemption. As mentioned in previous chapters, the purpose of Creation was that G-d have a dwelling among mortals,[2] and this dwelling is to be fashioned by man's efforts toward refining and bettering the world. For centuries, consciously and unconsciously, mankind has been busy constructing G-d's dwelling, and now it is emerging before our very eyes.

To explain by means of an analogy: A contractor is hired to build a complex mansion. From the moment he designs it, and throughout the building process, a clear picture of the final structure remains before his mind's eye. His workers may momentarily lose sight of the goal, yet as it takes shape, they too begin to envisage the edifice that their hands are transforming from a blueprint into reality. Indeed, as it nears completion, the building itself shows its builders the goal of their endeavors.

In our generation, at long last, mankind can begin to see the edifice, G-d's dwelling, which has been constructed through our efforts, and which will be consummated by the coming of *Mashiach*.

---

2.   *Midrash Tanchuma, Parshas Bechukosai*, sec. 3.

This relates to a classic concept of Jewish mysticism.[3] The Hebrew word for exile, *golah* (גולה), shares the same letters as the Hebrew word for redemption, *geulah* (גאולה), with one exception: *Geulah* possesses an *alef* (א) which stands for G-d, *alufo shel olam* ("the L-rd of the world").

The relationship between these two terms points to the essence of the Era of Redemption. All the material dimensions of our existence will continue in the Era of the Redemption; to quote Maimonides,[4] "There is no difference between the current age and the era of *Mashiach* except the subjugation [of Israel] to the [gentile] kingdoms."

What then will be unique about the Era of the Redemption? The *alef*, our awareness of G-d's presence. "The world will be filled with the knowledge of G-d as the waters cover the ocean bed;"[5] i.e., our perception of reality will be suffused with the knowledge of G-d.[6] The setting in which we live our lives will not change from the material to the miraculous. Rather, **we will change**; we will be more conscious of the G-dly life-force that permeates existence.

The above concept also points to the path which will hasten the coming of Redemption. Drawing down the *alef*, making the awareness of G-d part of our everyday experience, will prepare us for the era when the knowledge of G-d will be manifest in all aspects of existence.

---

3. *Vayikra Rabbah, Parshas Emor*, sec. 32; *Likkutei Torah, Behaalos'cha* 35c. See the development of this concept in *Sound the Great Shofar* (Kehot, 1992), pp. 54-55 and the sources noted there.
4. *Mishneh Torah, Hilchos Melachim* 12:2. See the explanation of this concept above in the essay entitled, "Will *Mashiach* Work Miracles?".
5. *Isaiah* 11:9, quoted in the *Mishneh Torah, Hilchos Melachim* 12:5.
6. To explain the simile involved: A vast multitude of creatures inhabit the ocean. Nevertheless, when looking at the ocean, what we see is the ocean as a whole, and not the particular entities it contains. Similarly, in the Era of the Redemption, although the material world will continue to exist, its existence will be suffused with an awareness of G-d.

As opposed to stable times when everything has a set place, times of transition like ours contain the potential for substantial growth and progress. Thus the present is a time of unique opportunity. By living with the Redemption, i.e., anticipating the knowledge, harmony, and peace of that era in our day-to-day lives, we can precipitate the time when these values will spread throughout the entire world, with the coming of *Mashiach*; may this take place in the immediate future.

Appendix A

The Laws of the King Mashiach by Maimonides[1]

[Since these two chapters (chaps. 11 and 12 of the Maimonides' *Hilchos Melachim*) have been referred to throughout the text, we have included a translation of them as they appear in the standard printed texts of the *Mishneh Torah*. The translation is taken from *I Await His Coming* (Kehot, N.Y., 1991) which presents analytical studies of these chapters, adapted from the works of the Lubavitcher Rebbe *Shlita*.]

---

1.   This title is used in some of the early printings of the *Mishneh Torah*.

CHAPTER ELEVEN

1. In future time, the King *Mashiach*² will arise and renew the Davidic dynasty, restoring it to its initial sovereignty. He will rebuild the *[Beis Ha]Mikdash* and gather in the dispersed remnant of Israel. Then, in his days, all the statutes will be reinstituted as in former times. We will offer sacrifices and observe the Sabbatical and Jubilee years according to all their particulars set forth in the Torah.

Whoever does not believe in him, or does not await his coming, denies not only [the statements of] the other prophets, but also [those of] the Torah and of Moshe, our teacher, for the Torah attests to his coming, stating:³

> And the L-rd your G-d will bring back your captivity and have compassion upon you. He will return and gather you [from among all the nations].... Even if your dispersed ones are in the furthest reaches of the heavens, [from there will G-d gather you in].... G-d will bring you [to the land]....

These explicit words of the Torah include all that was said [on the subject] by all the prophets.

There is also a reference [to *Mashiach*] in the passage concerning Bilaam, who prophesies about the two anointed [kings]: the first anointed [king],⁴ David, who saved Israel from her oppressors, and the final anointed [king] who will arise from

---

2.   In the original Heb., המלך המשיח (lit., "the anointed king"); i.e., the Messianic King.
3.   *Deuteronomy* 30:3-5.
4.   In the original Heb., the word here translated "anointed [king]" is simply המשיח (lit., "the anointed one"); i.e., the Messiah. It is used interchangeably with the earlier phrase.

among his descendants and save Israel [at the End of Days]. The following [quoted] phrases are from that passage:[5]

"I see it, but not now" — This refers to David; "I perceive it, but not in the near future" — This refers to King *Mashiach*.

"A star shall go forth from Yaakov" — This refers to David; "and a staff shall arise in Yisrael" — This refers to King *Mashiach*.

"He shall crush all of Moab's princes" — This refers to David, (as it is written,[6] "He smote Moab and measured them with a line"); "he shall break down all of Seth's descendants" — This refers to King *Mashiach*, (about whom it is written,[7] "He will rule from sea to sea").

"Edom will be demolished" — This refers to David, (as it is written,[8] "Edom became the servants of David"); "his enemy, Seir, will be destroyed" — This refers to King *Mashiach*, (as it is written,[9] "Saviors will ascend Mount Zion [to judge the mountain of Esau....]").

2.   Similarly, in regard to the Cities of Refuge, it is stated,[10] "When G-d will expand your borders... you shall add three more cities." This command has never been fulfilled. [Surely,] G-d did not give this command in vain, [and thus the intent was that it be fulfilled after the coming of *Mashiach*]. There is no need to cite prooftexts on the concept [of the *Mashiach*]

---

5.   *Numbers* 24:17-18.
6.   *II Samuel* 8:2.
7.   *Zechariah* 9:10.
8.   Cf. *II Samuel* 8:6 and 8:14.
9.   *Ovadiah* 1:21.
10.   *Deuteronomy* 19:8-9.

from the words of the prophets, for all [their] books are filled with it.

3. One should not entertain the notion that the King Mashiach must work miracles and wonders, bring about new phenomena within the world, resurrect the dead, or perform other similar deeds. This is [definitely] not true.

[A proof can be brought from the fact that] Rabbi Akiva, one of the greatest Sages of the Mishnah, was one of the supporters of King Ben Koziva, and would describe him as the King Mashiach. He and all the Sages of his generation considered him to be the King Mashiach until he was killed because of [his] sins. Once he was killed, they realized that he was not [the Mashiach]. The Sages did not ask him for any signs or wonders.

[Rather,] this is the main thrust of the matter: This Torah, with its statutes and laws, is everlasting. We may neither add to them nor detract from them.

4. If a king will arise from the House of David who delves deeply into the study of the Torah and, like David his ancestor, observes its mitzvos as prescribed by the Written Law and the Oral Law; if he will prevail upon all of Israel to walk in [the way of the Torah] and repair the breaches [in its observance]; and if he will fight the wars of G-d; — we may, with assurance, consider him Mashiach.

If he succeeds in the above, builds the [Beis Ha]Mikdash on its site, and gathers in the dispersed remnant of Israel, he is definitely the Mashiach.

He will then perfect the entire world, [motivating all the nations] to serve G-d together, as it is written,[11] "I will make the peoples pure of speech so that they will all call upon the Name of G-d and serve Him with one purpose."

CHAPTER TWELVE

1. One should not entertain the notion that in the Era of *Mashiach* any element of the natural order will be nullified, or that there will be any innovation in the work of creation. Rather, the world will continue according to its pattern.

Although Yeshayahu[12] states, "The wolf will dwell with the lamb, and the leopard will lie down with the young goat," these [words] are an allegory and a riddle. They mean that Israel will dwell securely together with the wicked gentiles who are likened to wolves and leopards, as in the verse,[13] "A wolf of the deserts despoils them, a leopard watches over their cities." [In this Era, all nations] will return to the true faith and no longer plunder or destroy. Instead, at peace with Israel, they will eat that which is permitted, as it is written,[14] "The lion shall eat straw like the ox."

Similarly, other prophecies of this nature concerning *Mashiach* are analogies. In the Era of the King *Mashiach*, everyone will realize what was implied by these metaphors and allusions.

---

11. *Zephaniah, loc. cit.*
12. *Isaiah* 11:6.
13. *Jeremiah* 5:6.
14. *Isaiah* 11:7.

2. Our Sages taught:[15] "There will be no difference between the current age and the Era of *Mashiach* except [our emancipation from] subjugation to the [gentile] kingdoms."

The simple meaning of the words of the prophets appears to imply that the War of Gog and Magog[16] will take place at the beginning of the Messianic Age. Before the War of Gog and Magog, a prophet will arise to rectify Israel's conduct and prepare their hearts [for the Redemption], as it is written:[17] "Behold, I am sending you Eliyah(u)[18] [the prophet, before the advent of the great and awesome Day of G-d]."

He will not come [in order] to declare the pure, impure, nor to declare the impure, pure; nor [will he come in order] to disqualify the lineage of those presumed to be of flawless descent, nor to validate lineage which is presumed to be blemished. Rather, [he will come in order] to establish peace in the world; as [the above prophecy] continues,[19] "He will bring back the hearts of the fathers to the children."

Some of the Sages say that Eliyahu will appear [immediately] before the coming of *Mashiach*.

All these and similar matters cannot be [clearly] known by man until they occur, for they are undefined in the words of the prophets. Even the Sages have no established tradition regarding these matters, beyond what is implied by the verses; hence there is a divergence of opinion among them.

In any case, neither the sequence of these events nor their precise details are among the fundamental principles of the faith. One should not occupy himself at length with the *aggadot*

---

15. *Berachos* 34b.
16. [*Ezekiel* ch. 38.]
17. *Malachi* 3:23.
18. [The name of the prophet is occasionally spelled, as in this verse, without the final letter *vav*.]
19. *Malachi* 3:24.

and *midrashim* that deal with these and similar matters, nor should he deem them of prime importance, for they bring one to neither the awe nor the love [of G-d].

Similarly, one should not try to calculate the appointed time [for the coming of *Mashiach*]. Our Sages declared:[20] "May the spirits of those who attempt to calculate the final time [of *Mashiach's* coming] expire!" Rather, one should await [his coming] and believe in the general conception of the matter, as we have explained.

3.   During the Era of the King *Mashiach,* once his kingdom has been established and all of Israel has gathered around him, the entire [nation's] line of descent will be established on the basis of his words, through the prophetic spirit which will rest upon him. As it is written,[21] "He shall sit as a refiner and purifier."

He will purify the lineage of the Levites first, stating that "This one is a priest of defined lineage" and "This one is a Levite of defined lineage." Those whose lineage he does not recognize will be relegated to the status of Israelites. This is implied by the following verse:[22] "The governor said to them, '[They shall not eat of the most holy things] until a priest arises [who will wear] the *Urim* and *Tumim.*' " From this verse one can infer that the genealogy of those presumed to be of unquestioned [priestly and levitical] lineage will be traced by means of the prophetic spirit, and those found to be of such lineage will be made known.

He will define the lineage of the Israelites according to their tribe alone; i.e., he will make known each person's tribal

---

20. *Sanhedrin* 97b.
21. *Malachi* 3:3.
22. *Ezra* 2:63.

origin, stating that "This one is from this tribe" and "This one is from another tribe." However, concerning a person who is presumed to be of unblemished lineage, he will not state that "He is illegitimate," or "He is of slave lineage," for the law rules that once a family has become intermingled [within the entire Jewish people], they may remain intermingled.

4. The Sages and prophets did not yearn for the Messianic Era in order that [the Jewish people] rule over the entire world, nor in order that they have dominion over the gentiles, nor that they be exalted by them, nor in order that they eat, drink and celebrate. Rather, their aspiration was that [the Jewish people] be free [to involve themselves] in Torah and its wisdom, without anyone to oppress or disturb them, and thus be found worthy of life in the World to Come, as we explained in *Hilchos Teshuvah*.

5. In that Era there will be neither famine nor war, neither envy nor competition, for good things will flow in abundance and all the delights will be as freely available as dust. The occupation of the entire world will be solely to know G-d. The Jews will therefore be great sages and know the hidden matters, and will attain an understanding of their Creator to the [full] extent of mortal potential; as it is written,[23] "For the world will be filled with the knowledge of G-d as the waters cover the ocean bed."

---

23. *Isaiah* 11:9.

APPENDIX B

OPEN YOUR EYES AND SEE
Attuning Oneself to a Changing Reality

An Adaptation of Addresses of
the Lubavitcher Rebbe שליט״א
on Shabbos Parshas Vayeitzei, 5752 and other occasions.

[Since we have frequently referred to statements of the Lubavitcher Rebbe *Shlita* regarding the imminence of the Redemption, we have included this essay adapted from his addresses, which highlights this theme. The essay is taken from *Sound the Great Shofar* (Kehot, N.Y., 1992).]

ISRAEL'S MISSION

Our Sages state,[1] "The world was created solely for *Mashiach.*" For G-d created the world so that He would have "a

---

1.   *Sanhedrin* 96b.

dwelling place among mortals,"[2] and this ideal will be realized in the Era of the Redemption. At that time the Divine Presence will become manifest in this world, for, in the words of Isaiah's promise,[3] "the earth will be filled with the knowledge of G-d as the waters cover the ocean bed."[4]

Since it is human nature to appreciate something for which one has worked far more than an unearned gift,[5] G-d desired that man have a share in bringing this promise to fruition, that he become G-d's partner in creation.[6] This indeed has been the purpose of the thousands of years during which the Jewish people have served G-d, thereby refining the world and preparing it for the manifestation of His Presence within it. Throughout the centuries, as we have wandered from country to country and from continent to continent, the inner purpose of these journeys has been to cultivate these places and prepare them for the Redemption.[7]

Throughout our history, our people have yearned for the consummation of this task, for the time when *Mashiach* will actually come. Three times a day, every day of the year, we ask G-d:[8] "May our eyes behold Your return to Zion in mercy."

---

2. *Midrash Tanchuma, Parshas Bechukosai*, sec. 3; *Tanya*, ch. 36.
3. The revelation of the Divine Presence is implied by the use of term "dwelling". Just as it is in a person's home that his personality finds expression without restraint or inhibition, it will be in this world that G-dliness will be revealed without restraint.
4. *Yeshayahu* 11:9; *Rambam, Mishneh Torah, Hilchos Melachim* 12:5.
5. Cf. *Bava Metzia* 38a.
6. *Shabbos* 10a, 119b; *Likkutei Sichos*, Vol. XV, p. 95.
7. See *Sound the Great Shofar* (Kehot, N.Y., 1992) essay entitled "Make *This* Place *Eretz Yisrael.*"

   The Sages teach (*Pesachim* 87b) that "The only reason for which G-d exiled the Jewish people among the nations of the world was that proselytes be added to them." In this teaching, *Chassidus* perceives an allusion to the ultimate cosmic mission of the Jewish people during their wanderings through the material universe — the task of sifting and elevating the exiled sparks of holiness that are embedded within it. See *MiGolah LiGeulah* (in English translation, published by Sichos In English), Part I, ch. 2, quoting *Sefer HaMaamarim 5702*, p. 69.
8. *Siddur Tehillat HaShem*, p. 58 *et al.*

Indeed, our Sages[9] teach us that one of the first questions a soul will be asked in its judgment for the afterlife is, "Did you anticipate the Redemption?"

OPEN YOUR EYES: THE TABLE IS SET FOR THE FEAST

The above assumes unique relevance in the present time, for the Jewish people have completed the mission with which G-d has charged us. To borrow an expression of the Previous Rebbe's,[10] we have already "polished the buttons": everything necessary to bring about the Redemption has already been accomplished.[11]

Our readiness for the Redemption is also reflected in the world at large. The values of freedom, tolerance, and generosity have spread throughout the community of nations. Regimes that have opposed them have toppled, giving way for greater communication and sharing.

Our Sages[12] have described the Redemption as a feast. To echo this analogy,[13] the table has already been set, everything has been served, and we are sitting at the table together with *Mashiach*. All we need to do is open our eyes.

---

9. *Shabbos* 31a.
10. *Sichah* of Simchas Torah, 5689 [1928].
11. See footnote 19 to the Overview to *Sound the Great Shofar*.

    Indeed, we learn that G-d will bring about the ultimate Redemption speedily even when the Jewish people have not yet fully cleansed themselves. For in the penitential prayers of *Selichos* (quoting *Tehillim* 25:22 and 130:8), we say, *first:* "G-d, redeem Israel from all his afflictions"; and *afterwards:* "And He will redeem Israel from all his sins." First G-d will redeem the Jews from their difficulties — including the greatest difficulty, the exile — and *then* He will redeem them from their sins. See the above essay entitled "Every Jew Has a Silver Lining."
12. *Pesachim* 119b.
13. See footnote 21 to the above Overview.

PREPARING THE WORLD FOR MASHIACH

In previous generations as well, there has always been a potential for the Redemption.[14] In the popular version of the *Rambam's* Thirteen Principles of Faith,[15] the twelfth Principle reads: "I believe with perfect faith in the coming of the *Mashiach*. Even if he delays, I will wait every day for him to come." As has been explained,[16] this does not mean that every day we should wait for *Mashiach's* ultimate coming, but that every day, we should wait expectantly for *Mashiach* to come *on that very day.*

Our Sages[17] describe *Mashiach* as waiting anxiously to come. In previous generations, however, his coming was prevented by the fact that the Jews had not completed the tasks expected of them. At present, however, those tasks have been accomplished; there is nothing lacking. All we have to do is accept *Mashiach.*

This is the challenge facing our generation: To make the world conscious of *Mashiach*, and to create an environment that will allow his mission to be fulfilled. Every element of our study of the Torah and our observance of its *mitzvos* should be permeated by this objective, and directed towards it.

---

14. Note the comments of the *Chasam Sofer* (Responsa on *Choshen Mishpat*, Vol. 6, Responsum 98), that in every generation, there is a potential *Mashiach*. Moreover, were there no obstacles which prevented his coming, he would have come already. See also *Sdei Chemed, Pe'as HaSadeh, Maareches Alef*, Principle 70.
15. The full text of these thirteen principles, which differs slightly from the popular version that appears in many *Siddurim*, is found in the *Rambam's* Commentary to the *Mishnah*, in the Introduction to ch. 10 of Tractate *Sanhedrin*.
16. *Likkutei Sichos*, Vol. XXIII, p. 394.
17. *Sanhedrin* 98a.

BECOMING ATTUNED TO THE REDEMPTION

We can gain awareness of *Mashiach* through the study of *pnimiyus HaTorah*,[18] the Torah's mystical dimensions, and in particular, through the study of the subjects of redemption and *Mashiach*.[19] This process will open the eyes of our mind, so that as we live our lives day by day, we will remain constantly attuned to the concept of redemption.

Furthermore, the increase in our awareness of the nature of the Redemption will serve as a catalyst, which will hasten the coming of the day when we can actually open our eyes and see — that we are in *Eretz Yisrael*, and in Jerusalem, and, indeed, in the *Beis HaMikdash*, with the coming of the Redemption.

May this be realized in the immediate future.

---

18. The connection between *pnimiyus HaTorah* and the Era of the Redemption is emphasized by the Baal Shem Tov in the renowned letter in which he describes an encounter with *Mashiach* in the spiritual realms. He asked *Mashiach*, "When are you coming?" And *Mashiach* answered him, "When the wellsprings of your teachings shall spread outward." (See the above Overview, and footnotes 12-14 there.)

    Since the essence of *Mashiach's* coming is to allow for "the earth to be filled with the knowledge of G-d," it will be heralded by the spreading of *pnimiyus HaTorah*, which disseminates this knowledge.

    Such study is not the exclusive province of men. The obligation of women to likewise study the inner dimensions of the Torah, i.e., the teachings of *Chassidus*, is explained by the Rebbe *Shlita* in *Sefer HaMinhagim* (English translation; Kehot, N.Y., 1991), p. 192. See also the essay entitled "A Woman's Place in Torah" (*Sichos In English*, Vol. 45, pp. 16-22).

19. This should include the study of these subjects not only in *pnimiyus HaTorah*, but also as they are explained in Torah law, for example, the final two chapters of the *Mishneh Torah* of the *Rambam*. In-depth analyses of these texts by the Rebbe *Shlita*, both on the level of *halachah* and of *Chassidus*, are to be found in *I Await His Coming Every Day* (Kehot, N.Y., 1991).

APPENDIX C

SOUND THE GREAT SHOFAR
Togetherness — Between Individuals,
and Within Individuals

An Adaptation of Addresses of the
Lubavitcher Rebbe שליט"א, on the 24th of Adar Rishon
and on Shabbos Parshas Vayakhel, 5752

[This essay, adapted from the last public address the
Lubavitcher Rebbe *Shlita* delivered before suffering a stroke in
1992, focuses on the importance of developing inner harmony
and establishing unity with others, as catalysts for the
Redemption. The essay appears in the book bearing the same
title.]

MORE THAN A GEOGRAPHIC INGATHERING

> Sound the great *shofar* for our freedom; raise a banner to
> gather our exiles, and bring us together from the four
> corners of the earth into our land.[1]

Three times a day we express this fervent wish — that
Mashiach come and gather our people to *Eretz Yisrael*, the eternal heritage of our people.[2] This involves more than a mere
geographic movement on the part of our people. At that time
G-d will "bring us together" and establish unity among us, for
in that age, the Era of the Redemption,[3] "there will be neither
famine nor war, neither envy nor competition."

The events of recent years point to the imminence of that
era; many signs of the Redemption are appearing. The won-
drous ingathering of hundreds of thousands of Jews to *Eretz
Yisrael* is surely an obvious harbinger of the ultimate ingathering of our dispersed nation. Surging waves of migration that
stand out boldly in our nation's history are now reaching our
holy land, including hundreds of thousands of people who were
forcibly held back for decades.[4] Indeed, the very nations which
had previously blocked their emigration are now granting them
permission and even assistance to settle in *Eretz Yisrael*.[5]

---

1. Daily liturgy, *Siddur Tehillat HaShem*, p. 55.
2. Note *Rambam, Mishneh Torah, Hilchos Melachim* 11:4, which specifies the
   ingathering of the dispersed remnants of Israel as one of the principal indicators
   by which the coming of the Redemption can be ascertained.
3. *Rambam, op. cit.,* 12:5.
4. Needless to say, settling the vast hosts of immigrants in *Eretz Yisrael* requires
   massive resources. It is a unique privilege and responsibility to help meet this
   challenge, and offer substantial assistance. (See the address of the Rebbe *Shlita*
   to the participants in the Machne Israel Development Fund, in *Sichos In English*,
   Vol. 47, pp. 216-221.)
5. Unfortunately, there are still isolated countries that prevent Jews from emigrat-
   ing. Nevertheless, the successful immigration of the many Jews who have
   reached *Eretz Yisrael* will generate spiritual influences that will facilitate the
   immigration of their brethren. See the *maamar* entitled *Amar R. Oshia 5739*

INTEGRATING A FRAGMENTED PERSONALITY

Together with the foretaste of the Redemption that we have been granted, we have also been given the potential to anticipate the Redemption and incorporate the spiritual ideals of that era within our everyday life. In this vein, the concept of gathering in the dispersed has relevance within every individual's personal world, and likewise within the sphere of our relations with others.

It is not only a nation that stands in need of ingathering. In our time, we often encounter fragmented personalities, people who find difficulty integrating their various drives and motivations. The source for this centrifugal thrust lies in a lack of coordination within our multifaceted spiritual makeup. We have ten different potentials[6] and we have been given an ongoing, lifelong task of establishing harmony between them.

This endeavor is illustrated in a renowned chassidic story: Reb Zalman Aharon, the elder son of the Rebbe Maharash, once asked his uncle, Reb Yosef Yitzchak, if he recited his prayers *betzibbur*, "with the community." Reb Yosef Yitzchak answered in the affirmative. The very next day, however, Reb Zalman Aharon noticed that his uncle prolonged his prayers, lingering far longer than any congregation would.

"Didn't you tell me you prayed *betzibbur?*" he asked.

"I do," his uncle replied. "*Betzibbur* literally means 'with the collective.' After I marshall together the ten components of my soul, I pray."

(published in *Sefer HaMaamarim — Melukat*, Vol. IV, p. 89), which explains a similar pattern of spiritual causality.

6. These ten qualities in turn further subdivide, producing the full range of emotional attributes. See *Tanya*, ch. 3, and "Mystical Concepts in Chassidus," by R. Jacob Immanuel Schochet, ch. 3, sec. 6 (Kehot, N.Y. 1988).

A BOND ABOVE CONSCIOUS THOUGHT

How is such a unity established? How can a person bring the divergent thrusts of his personality into harmony? — Through dedicating them to G-d. When a person makes an all-encompassing commitment to G-d, he gains a wholesome sense of fulfillment[7] that enables him to establish harmony among the diverse elements of his being.

The unity established is not manufactured, but rather reflects the inner truth of every person's being. For the soul is[8] "an actual part of G-d from above." Consequently, all of its potentials reflect this fundamental G-dly core.

This process of establishing internal harmony is reflected in the very first statement a Jew makes upon rising: *Modeh Ani* — "I gratefully acknowledge..."[9] What is the core of this declaration? — That immediately upon awakening, a person gathers together his entire being and devotes it to G-d.

To explain: Seemingly, before a person is able to make such a declaration, he should consciously perceive G-d's presence. This in turn would appear to require that he contemplate the world around him until he comes to the realization that[10] "the entire earth is filled with His glory." Only then would he be able to make an all-encompassing commitment to G-d.

We, however, do not need such preparation, for our connection with G-dliness is intrinsic and constant, shaping our thinking processes even when we sleep. Indeed, a person's bond with G-d may be even greater when he sleeps than when he is awake, for then his conscious intellectual faculties do not con-

---

7. In a related context, the Maggid of Mezritch offers a non-literal interpretation of the phrase (*Numbers* 10:1) *shnei chatzotzros,* (lit., "two trumpets"), rendering it as *shnei chatzi tzuros,* "two half-entities." A Jew and G-d are both "half-entities" until a union is established between them.
8. *Tanya,* ch. 2, paraphrasing *Job* 31:2.
9. *Siddur Tehillat HaShem,* p. 6.
10. *Isaiah* 6:3.

trol his thoughts. In their absence, his essence can surface. And the essence of every soul is connected with G-d at all times.[11]

When a person rises from sleep, however, he becomes conscious of himself as an individual entity, and indeed, as a powerful entity. Nevertheless, as soon as he becomes aware of his own existence, he gives himself over to G-d with thankful acknowledgment.[12] And this enables him to perceive how[9] "great is Your faithfulness," i.e., how every entity in the world reflects G-d's gracious kindness.

UNCONDITIONAL LOVE

Thus the establishment of harmony and unity within our individual beings enables us to perceive the inner unity that pervades the totality of existence.[13] Similarly, it enhances our ability to establish unity in our relations with others.

The importance of such efforts is emphasized by the fact that the Alter Rebbe placed the declaration,[14] "I hereby undertake the fulfillment of the mitzvah, 'Love your fellowman as yourself,' " at the very beginning of the prayer service, making it the foundation of all of one's daily activities.

In simple terms, this command means that when one person sees another, he should try to unite with him, for in truth all men share the same inner G-dly essence. When a person appreciates this fundamental commonalty, he understands that

11. Note the explanation of the *Rambam* in *Hilchos Gerushin* 2:20.
12. In the *Mishneh Torah, Hilchos Teshuvah* 3:4, the *Rambam* speaks of "those who slumber in the vanities of worldly existence." The fundamental unity all men share with G-d affects these individuals, despite their "sleep". Accordingly, their "slumber" will surely be only temporary. Ultimately, they too will "wake up" and develop a conscious relationship with G-d.
13. In this vein, our Sages (*Berachos* 13b) — and this is quoted as *halachah* (*Shulchan Aruch, Orach Chayim* 61:6, *Shulchan Aruch HaRav* 61:6) — interpret the expression "G-d is one" in the *Shema* as meaning, not only that there is one G-d, but also that His oneness permeates every element of existence.
14. *Siddur Tehillat HaShem*, p. 12, quoting *Leviticus* 19:18.

the various differences that exist between people need not lead to division. On the contrary, they enable each person to complement the other and contribute an element which is lacking, or not as developed, in the other's personality.

This thrust toward unity applies not only to those individuals in one's immediate community, but to all people, even those far removed; indeed, even those in a distant corner of the world. Needless to say, the manner in which these feelings of unity are expressed will differ in terms of the practical means of expression available, but the feelings of oneness are universal in nature.

FOCUSING ON OUR SHARED CONNECTION

Even when the distance between individuals is also spiritual in nature, i.e., when one person does not share another's level of adherence to Torah law, *one should persistently focus on the essential connection which is shared*, and not on the differences.

In regard to one's *own* personal conduct, one must emphasize two modes of serving G-d, striving both to[15] "Turn away from evil, and [to] do good." When, however, one relates to another individual, one must channel one's energies solely in the path of[16] "Do[ing] good." The emphasis on a person's positive qualities will, moreover, encourage their expression, for[17] "a little light dispels much darkness."

---

15. *Psalms* 34:15.
16. When he was four years old, the Rebbe Rayatz asked his father why we need two eyes.

   Replied the Rebbe Rashab, "With his right eye one should look at a *Siddur* and at a fellow Jew; with his left eye one should look at sweets and toys." (*Sefer HaToldos* of the Rebbe Rayatz, Vol. I, pp. 8-9.)
17. *Tanya*, ch. 12; cf. *Tzeidah LaDerech*, sec. 12.

Although there are times when another individual's conduct warrants reproof,[18] before speaking one should question whether he himself is fit to be the one to administer it. Furthermore, if reproof must be given, it should be offered gently,[19] which will obviously enable it to be accepted more readily than harsh speech. Moreover, such words should be spoken only on select occasions.

These concepts are reflected in the verse,[20] "One who withholds the rod hates his son," which indicates that stiff rebuke may be given only when the relationship between two individuals is like a father and a son. There are two concepts implied by this verse: Firstly, that to give rebuke, one must love the other person just as a father loves his child; secondly, that the difference in level between the two people must be as radical as that between a father and a son. This is not true in most cases. Since all individuals share a fundamental equality, it is appropriate that people relate to each other as equals.

GIVING OF ONESELF

The unity that we share with others should not remain merely in the realm of feeling, but should be translated into actual deeds of love and kindness. In regard to the sacrifices that were brought in the *Beis HaMikdash*, it is written,[21] "A person who shall bring from you...." The Alter Rebbe[22] notes that seemingly it would have been more proper to say, "A person of

---

18. See *Shulchan Aruch, Orach Chayim* 608:2; *Shulchan Aruch HaRav*, sec. 156 and 308.

19. *Rambam, Mishneh Torah, Hilchos De'os* 6:8. See also the essays entitled: "The Innate Quality of Every Jew — The Indivisibility of the Land of Israel" (published in *Sichos In English*, Vol. 44, pp. 206-209); "Every Jew has a Silver Lining" (*ibid.*, Vol. 47, pp. 11-18); and "The Safest Place in the World" (*ibid.*, pp. 19-24).

20. *Proverbs* 13:24.

21. *Leviticus* 1:2.

22. *Likkutei Torah, Parshas Vayikra*. These concepts are quoted in many later chassidic teachings as well. See *Basi LeGani 5710* (translated into English by Sichos In English, 5750).

you who shall bring...." The transposition of the words in the verse, however, indicates that the offering must be "from you," of a person's own self.

A similar concept applies in regard to *tzedakah*. One should not give merely what is left over after one has taken care of one's own needs, but should give "from you," from one's own self. And these gifts should be substantial. To borrow the words of a verse,[23] "everything a person owns he will give for the sake of his life." Similarly, the realization of the fundamental unity we share with others will prompt us to give generously, without limits.

Moreover, our gifts to *tzedakah* should constantly be increased. Every moment, the creation as a whole is being renewed[24] and is receiving additional blessings through G-d's benevolence. Therefore, at every moment, we should renew and increase our commitment to *tzedakah*, amplifying the manner in which we help others.

"BLESS US, ...ALL AS ONE"

Unity is the key to G-d's blessings. Thus, in our daily prayers, we say *"Bless us, our Father, all as one."* The teachings of *Chassidus*[25] explain that the very fact of being together "all as one," makes us worthy of blessing. And this unity will lead to the ultimate blessing — the coming of the time when G-d will "sound the great *shofar*," and together[26] "with our youth and with our elders... with our sons and with our daughters," the entire Jewish people will proceed to *Eretz Yisrael*, to Jerusalem,

---

23. *Job* 2:4. In *Tanya, Iggeres HaKodesh*, ch. 3, the Alter Rebbe explains that although our Sages prescribe that a person should not give more than a fifth of his resources to *tzedakah*, there are certain situations when a person can — and indeed should — transcend these limits.
24. *Tanya, Shaar HaYichud VeHaEmunah*, ch. 1.
25. *Tanya*, ch. 32.
26. *Exodus* 10:9.

and to the Third *Beis HaMikdash*. May this take place in the immediate future.

GLOSSARY

ayin — lit., nothingness. In Chassidic terminology, the term is used to refer to a state of non-being that serves as a contrast to true existence.

Baal Shem Tov — (lit., "Master of the Good Name"): Rabbi Yisrael ben Eliezar (1698-1760), founder of Chassidism.

Chabad — An acronym for the Hebrew words meaning "wisdom, understanding, and knowledge." The approach to Chassidism which filters its spiritual and emotional power through the intellect. A synonym for *Chabad* is Lubavitch, the name of the town where this movement flourished.

Chafetz Chayim — (lit., "He who desires life"): Rabbi Yisrael Meir Kagan, one of the foremost Rabbinical figures of the European Jewish community before World War II. Called *Chafetz Chayim* because of his renown text of that title.

Chassidism — The approach to orthodox Judaism founded by the Baal Shem Tov which stresses emotional involvement in prayer, the power of joy, the love for every Jew, and an awareness of mystic knowledge.

Elijah, the prophet — A historical figure in the Bible, see *I Kings*, ch. 17-22, *II Kings*, ch. 1-2. According to the narrative in *II Kings*, ch. 2, he did not die, but rather rose into heaven. Tradition maintains that he descends to our material world from time to time and reveals himself to the righteous. Ultimately, it will be he who will announce the coming of the Messiah (see *Malachi* 3:23).

Era of the Redemption — The Messianic Age.

Eretz Yisrael — The land of Israel.

geulah — The Hebrew word for "redemption."

golah — The Hebrew word for "exile."

Ikvesa diMeshicha — The time directly before the Messianic Age when *Mashiach's* approaching footsteps can already be heard.

Kabbalah — (lit., the received tradition): The Jewish mystic tradition.

Rav Aryeh Levine — One of the foremost Rabbinic leaders in *Eretz Yisrael* from the 1930's to the 1960's.

Lubavitch — (lit., "town of love"): The town in White Russia which served as the center of *Chabad* Chassidism from 1813 to 1915 and whose name has become synonymous with the movement.

Lubavitcher Rebbe *Shlita* — The present Lubavitcher Rebbe, Rabbi Menachem Mendel Schneerson (b. 1902), the leader of the *Chabad* Chassidic movement today.

Maimonides — Rabbi Moshe ben Maimon, also referred to as the *Rambam* (1135-1204). One of the foremost Jewish thinkers of the Middle Ages. His *Mishneh Torah* is one of the classic texts of Jewish law, and his *Guide to the Perplexed*, one of the classics of Jewish philosophy.

Mashiach — (lit., "the anointed one"): the Messiah.

mashpia — (lit., "source of influence"): In Chassidic circles, a spiritual mentor.

Mishneh Torah — Maimonides' classic text of Jewish law.

Midrash — The classical collection of the Sages' homiletical teachings on the Bible.

mitzvah, pl. *mitzvos* — (lit., "command"): a religious precept, one of the Torah's 613 commandments.

Previous Rebbe — Rabbi Yosef Yitzchak Schneersohn (1880-1950). The sixth Lubavitcher Rebbe, who headed the movement's fight against the Communist oppression of religion in Russia and who transferred the movement to the U.S. during World War II.

Rabbi Shneur Zalman of Liadi — (1745-1812), the founder of the *Chabad* Chassidic movement. Author of the *Tanya*, a classic text of the Chassidic tradition, and *Shulchan Aruch HaRav*, one of the important texts of Jewish law.

Rebbe — (lit., "teacher" or "master"): A realized Torah leader who serves as a spiritual guide to a following of Chassidim.

Shabbos — The Sabbath.

shtetl — (lit., "village"): the basic living unit of the Jewish community in Eastern Europe.

Talmud — The basic compendium of Jewish law, thought, and Biblical commentary, comprising the *Mishnah* and the *Gemara*. When unspecified refers to the Babylonian Talmud edited in the end of the fifth century C.E.

tziruf — Literally, the process of smelting ore, an analogy for the spiritual task of refining the world.

yesh — (lit., "it is"). In Chassidic terminology "being," and ultimately "true being."

Yiddish — Lit. "Jewish." The dialect of German spoken by the Jews that became their mother tongue.

Zohar — (lit., "radiance"): the classic text of the *Kabbalah*.

Dedicated by the Chassan

Moshe Malamud

In Memory of his Grandparents Whose Imprint
on His Life Is Lovingly Remembered

❦

In Memory of

Reb Shlomo ben Reb Yechiel
Malamud

Who lived a long life, replete with the study of the Torah and
the observance of its mitzvos. Those who knew him,
particularly his children and grandchildren, gained
inspiration from him, motivating them to deeper Jewish
commitment and observance.

Passed away the 19th of Iyar, 5753

and in Memory of

Sarah Rachel bas Reb Shmuel Yoel HaKohen
Malamud

A woman of valor,
and devoted to her children and grandchildren.

Passed away the 29th of Shevat, 5732

❦

In Memory of

Reb Yisroel ben Moshe
Schneid

A man of faith and deed, tzedakah and kindness,
who sought every opportunity for acts of charity.
An example for his children and grandchildren,
showing them both metchlechkeit and yiddishkeit.

Passed away the 8th of Teves, 5745

In honor of

Moshe and Elke שיחיו Malamud

On the occasion of their Marriage
Sunday, 8th Day of Tammuz, 5753

❧

dedicated by their parents

Mr. & Mrs. Shmuel Yechiel & Rosalynn שיחיו Malamud

Rabbi & Mrs. Yankel & Chana Devorah שיחיו Pinson

and by their grandparents

Mrs. Helen שתחי' Schneid

Mr. & Mrs. Dovid & Sarah שיחיו Deitsch

Rabbi & Mrs. Yehoshua שיחיו Pinson